ADVANCE PRAISE

"Dan Bongino walked away because he is an American patriot and the embodiment of the highest standards of honor, integrity, and character . . . exactly what we need inside the bubble."

— *Allen B. West, Lieutenant Colonel (US Army, Ret.),*
Member of 112th Congress

"For Dan Bongino to leave the Secret Service to fight the permanent political class could not have been easy, but his bravery is easily one of the reasons why Americans are learning more about how the D.C. "Bubble" grows but never pops."

— *Matthew Boyle, Investigative Journalist,* Breitbart News

"Real American heroes don't come out of Hollywood or the NFL; they come in the form of courageous Americans who do the 'Right Thing' solely because it is a matter of conscience for them. Dan Bongino is one of those who stood boldly for truth out of a sense of patriotism even when he knew that he would pay a price; and he did. This book tells his story and is an inspiration for the readers."

— *Lt. Gen. Jerry Boykin, former U.S. Deputy*
Undersecretary of Defense for Intelligence

LIFE INSIDE THE BUBBLE

DAN BONGINO

LIFE INSIDE THE BUBBLE

WHY A TOP-RANKED SECRET SERVICE AGENT WALKED AWAY FROM IT ALL

 WND Books

LIFE INSIDE THE BUBBLE

WND Books, Inc.
Washington, D.C.

Book designed by Mark Karis

WND Books are distributed to the trade by:
Midpoint Trade Books
27 West 20th Street, Suite 1102
New York, New York 10011

WND Books are available at special discounts for bulk purchases. WND Books, Inc.,
also publishes books in electronic formats. For more information call
(541) 474-1776 or visit www.wndbooks.com.

First Edition

Hardcover ISBN: 978-1-938067-36-5
eBook ISBN: 978-1-938067-37-2

Library of Congress information available

Printed in the United States of America
10 9 8 7 6 5 4 3 2 1

This book is dedicated to my wife Paula and my daughters Isabel and Amelia. It is the unconditional love they have shown me that fuels my fire and their safety net of support that has allowed me to leap.

CONTENTS

FOREWORD

AFTER SERVING ALMOST THREE DECADES with the Central Intelligence Agency in some of the most unique and dangerous capacities of clandestine and covert operations, my life often depended upon what the author of this book correctly describes as strength and character. I have discovered through personal experience and by witnessing terrorist threats worldwide that character and training are keys to the success not only of civilian intelligence agencies like the CIA but to personal security details of all branches of government. And the elite of the personal security world is, without a doubt, the Presidential

Protective Division of the United States Secret Service.

Dan Bongino served with the PPD for five years, and in *Life Inside the Bubble*, he gives the readers a very personal insight and understanding of the strength, courage, and conviction it takes to be the best of the best in the US Secret Service. The discipline to become a member, whether serving on the presidential detail or with the Uniformed Division, is not for the cerebrally weak or those with a flawed character. It is a very special individual who can perform the demanding tasks required, one who is physically and mentally disciplined, ethical, adaptive, and flexible. The character strengths of those working for the Secret Service should be the blueprint for other federal agencies.

Like many who reside in the state of Maryland, I became aware of Dan when he was a new political force within the local Republican Party, establishing himself as a future conservative star just before his incredible run for office in 2012. As I listened to his strong approach on drug policy reform, criminal justice reform, and fiscal policy, I immediately wanted to understand just who this man was and where he came from. *Life Inside the Bubble* delivers on that count—and many more.

The events Dan refers to in this book are true, from his childhood years attempting to understand life's unpredictable and sometimes violent path to protecting the most powerful men and women in the world. It is impossible to read this book and not come away with a feeling of elation, knowing that only in America can you grow up in a humble, uncertain environment, only to one day find yourself as one of the faces of hope for America's future.

Wayne Simmons CIA (ret.)
July 2013

PROLOGUE

THERE WAS A RECRUITING POSTER in the Secret Service headquarters during my time there that showed a number of steely-eyed agents surrounding the presidential limo as it drove down Pennsylvania Avenue. Above the picture the tagline read, "Some grow up wanting to be the president and some grow up wanting to protect the president." It was a clever line, playing on every young boy's desire to be the cop in a game of cops and robbers. The Secret Service is populated with dedicated men and women, largely attracted to the job because of the purity of the mission: keep the president safe. Agents agree to sacrifice themselves for the safety of the president regardless of his politics or his demeanor. The job requires incredibly long hours, at times in extreme conditions, and a commitment to live your life shadowing someone else while asking your family to understand the extreme sacrifice you may have to make and to temporarily live without you while you travel with the president.

The incredible weight of responsibility that accompanies every Secret Service agent, and specifically those in the Presidential Protective Division, has a tendency to distract agents from the outside world. Politics—whether those of the president you protect, or your feelings about the economy or foreign affairs—take a backseat to the daily rigors of the job. This distraction serves a purpose, as it keeps the agents' personal feelings about those they protect relatively ambivalent. Although I am certain that the strong character and unwavering dedication of the agents I worked with during my time with the Secret Service would never allow them to inject their personal or political beliefs into their job performance, it never hurts to believe in the man you are protecting. To believe in his leadership abilities and his policy prescriptions for a better tomorrow always serves as an added bonus.

After witnessing the endless political games across two presidential administrations while I served as a Secret Service agent, I knew I had to make a decision. It was unfair to the president and the Secret Service to become distracted, even for a moment. But it was becoming more and more difficult to accompany the president and listen to another speech whose content was contrary to the principles I believe make this country exceptional. The speeches ran contrary to everything in America's history that makes us incomparable as a nation, and to the principles we need in our future to maintain our unique position as a beacon of liberty and prosperity. I gave the Secret Service everything I had to give, and although I was deeply disturbed by the tone and direction of President Obama's speeches, I did not want to send the wrong message by resigning while assigned to his security detail. Compounding the problem was the trust the Secret Service placed in me. I was the top-ranked agent on my operational shift and was consistently assigned to conduct the security advances for presidential visits with the greatest degree of difficulty. To leave abruptly was sure to create a stir that I desperately wanted to avoid.

I decided the best path was to reapply myself during my remaining time with the president's security detail but to start looking for alternate paths for the next phase of my life. I loved my position at the Secret Service and was well aware of the dismal job market created by the economic recession. Giving it all up—the badge I proudly wore, the goodwill I built in over a decade of dedicated service, and the security of employment with a prestigious law-enforcement agency—was the toughest decision my wife and I were ever going to make. Despite the consequences, we knew it was time for a change. We both understood that there is a point in everyone's life where you must make a tough choice and follow your passion. Having seen the dark underbelly of Washington, DC, politics, we chose to take a risky step forward and do our best to affect change for the better.

My path into politics had a clear mission: to sound the alarm on what I had learned living inside the "DC bubble" by highlighting the very real consequences of an ever-expanding government and its insulated bureaucracy. My intent is not to criticize or minimize the efforts of the many government employees who are motivated by a genuine desire to serve. From my experience, any talk of bold change, transparency, and innovative new models of operation are typically pushed aside for incremental fixes. Sadly, our government prefers small Band-Aids to major surgery, even when the wounds are gaping. This book will take you through my journey and my experience with select people inside the bubble who displayed incomparable character and dignity and some who did not. In the closing chapters, I will share my insider perspective on the Fast and Furious investigation, the terrorist attacks on the Benghazi diplomatic mission and CIA annex, and the Boston Marathon terror attack. You will determine for yourself if the ongoing problems we have seen in law-enforcement investigations, counterterrorism, and international security are the result of a broken system or of the failing of our current leader's principles and governing philosophy.

ACKNOWLEDGMENTS

THERE ARE MANY PEOPLE TO THANK who helped light the path described in this book but none as important as my wife, Paula. Paula watched me struggle to find my path during my final months with the Secret Service. Watching me question everything was as painful for her as it was for me, and the decision to leave everything behind would never have been possible without her steadfast support. We knew we were doing the right thing, but in retrospect, I am still in awe of the sacrifice she was willing to make to support me. Her courage is inspirational to me and fuels the emotion in my words as I continue to travel and speak to various groups.

I would also like to thank my parents, John and Judy. Although their marriage struggled, their love for me and my two brothers, Joseph and Jim, never did. That my brothers and I have managed to remain standing despite the powerful headwinds of life seemingly always trying to blow us down is a testament to the power of the love our parents had for us. Although the book's painful recount of my earlier years may leave the reader with the impression of a painful childhood, my early years left me with love to spare. And, although our relationship has been contentious at times, I am grateful that Joseph, his wife Jonel, and Jim and his wife Jordana have always been there to support me when I've made tough decisions.

No book of this type could ever be complete without acknowledging the dedication and honor of the men and women of the United States Secret Service. At no point in this book are any security details revealed, and any information that may have compromised ongoing security operations was intentionally omitted. I deliberately wrote the book this way to ensure that no agent would ever have to modify a security template due to an idea fomented by this book. The men and women of the Secret Service are a quiet lot that perform a noble mission: keep the president alive no matter his politics, race, gender, success, or failure, and if, heaven forbid, something were to endanger his life, then you will die first. That is a profound level of commitment when one reflects on it, yet the men and women of the Secret Service rarely give it a second thought.

Having spent my twelve years with the Secret Service working with a number of military units that range from communications to medical to Special Forces, I also feel it necessary to extend the servicemen and women of our country a sincere debt of gratitude. For security reasons I intentionally omitted some of the more telling interactions I had with the men and women of our United States military, but I assure you they will never be omitted from my mind. Their bravery and selflessness is a testament to what makes this country peerless on the international stage. I was consistently humbled by being among our nation's finest warriors and want to again say, "Thank you; our freedom is your gift."

Growing up in a household where my parents were separated and my mother worked full time meant it was a challenge at times to find an ear willing to listen when I needed someone with whom to share my feelings. My grandmothers Eileen and Anne were always filling in those gaps and providing sage advice and guidance. Their love for me was boundless and I yearned to make them proud. I also found comfort in the homes of my three aunts: Eileen, Jane, and Susan. They all lived within blocks of our Queens, New York, apartment and subsequent home, and they were quick to provide a hot meal, a warm bed, or a shoulder to cry on when our situation at home was troubled.

Although I don't remember much about my grandfather Clifford, I know his impact on the community he lived in was dramatic. I wish I had more memories of him to relish. I do however have vivid memories of my grandfather Frank. He was my hero. He was a quiet man whose silent strength changed my life. The saddest day of my life was the day I lost him. A piece of me died with him that day.

Running a grassroots political campaign, such as the one I did in Maryland in 2012, requires the passionate dedication of thousands of volunteers and supporters. I want to thank every volunteer who showed up to wave a sign or knock on a door with me. I was consistently humbled by the number of people willing to stand in triple-degree heat with me and fight for a better tomorrow. I want to extend an additional thank-you to Jim for managing the campaign, Sharon for organizing the chaos, Kelly for believing in me, Maria and Ally for never giving up, and Brian, Mike, Jim, Marcia, Mark, and JoAnn for their time commitment.

Like many Americans, I have grown increasingly frustrated by the wall that has been built between the American people and their elected representatives. With trust in politicians at historic lows, it was refreshing to me, during my campaign, to encounter people who are guided by principle. I want to thank Senator Mike Lee from Utah for taking a chance on me when I had nothing but a passion for change. Senator Lee is that rare elected official who cares little for politics but cares greatly for a better tomorrow, and I will be forever grateful for his support and guidance. I also want to thank former congressman Lieutenant Colonel Allen West and former Republican nominee for vice president and former governor of Alaska Sarah Palin. They supported me because they believed in me, and in a political world driven by backroom deals and illicit pacts, it is refreshing to know that there are people out there who care more about a prosperous future than an immediate payoff.

No acknowledgement section would be complete without a heartfelt thank you to Lynda McLaughlin, the production team, and Sean Hannity for allowing me to amplify my message on Sean's show. As with Senator Lee, they took a chance on me, which I will never forget.

1

EARLY YEARS

GROWING UP ON ROSE LANE in Smithtown, New York, with my mother, Judy, my father, John, and my two brothers, Jim and Joseph, was quiet, peaceful, and relatively unmemorable for all of the right reasons. We made the short walk each morning to our school, Forest Brook Elementary, at the end of our street. My father was a building inspector and licensed plumber and my mother worked in a supermarket. They provided for a comfortable and peaceful existence. All of this was about to change for us, and when the change appeared it came swiftly, with no harbinger of what our future would hold.

My father and mother were very good at hiding the trouble in their marriage. They rarely fought openly, so from an eight-year-old's perspective everything appeared normal. Their marriage began to fracture during the early 1980s and by 1983 was a marriage in name only. By my ninth birthday I understood what was happening. I distinctly remember a fight that resulted in a bottle of Fox's U-Bet chocolate syrup shattering on the front porch and creating a huge, dark stain. The memory is distinct and fresh to this day. With their divorce moving forward, my mother could no longer afford our Smithtown home and decided it was time to move back to Queens, New York. She was raised in Queens, and although she may have been accustomed to the rigors of city life, my brothers and I definitely were not.

The new apartment in Queens was located on Myrtle Avenue, above the bar my grandfather owned. My mother had little money and the bitter divorce proceedings dragged on, so her salary from working in the supermarket across the street was our only means of support. The bar attracted few customers since my grandfather's passing years earlier. My mother and her three sisters attempted to manage it with little success, and living above it was a stressful experience. In addition to the noise from the jukebox every night, the apartment was small, cramped, and infested with rats. Myrtle Avenue was always crowded with cars and people in no rush to contribute to the night's silence.

My mother started seeing a man she knew from her childhood not long after moving back to the old neighborhood. Mike, or as she had us refer to him, "Big Mike," was a grizzled dockworker and a former boxer. He was a physically imposing figure at six feet, five inches and nearly 280 pounds. His demeanor was very different from than of the father we left behind in Smithtown, and growing accustomed to his increasing presence at the small apartment was a difficult adjustment for my brothers and me.

Mike was generally a decent man, but he became an entirely different person when he drank. He grew up in the hard city streets where fighting was the rule rather than the exception. Having known nothing but peace in my childhood to this point, constantly hearing about violence and fighting was beginning to affect me. After our first year in the apartment, Mike moved in with us and became a permanent fixture in our lives. I was unaware, at this point, of the consequences of crossing Mike, but I quickly learned the boundaries of our relationship. Sitting in the kitchen one night, Big Mike asked me in front of my mother if I would like to join him and his son Mike at the Ridgewood Grove Arena to watch WWF wrestling. Having no interest, I replied, half-jokingly, "I have other things to do." These words would come back to haunt me the next morning when he furiously screamed at me about my rudeness while I was lying in bed. I was stunned and scared, and I learned never to speak to him again in any way that could even be perceived as rude. This was just a small hint of what was to come.

I awoke in the middle of the night a couple of weeks later and heard muffled screams, the kind of screams that have to be muffled. Thinking I was having a nightmare I closed my eyes, but the sound would not relent. My brother Joseph, six at the time, made the mistake of crossing Mike earlier that day for a reason most rational adults would attribute to childhood immaturity. Mike had been drinking and decided that Joseph was going to be the release valve for his rage. This was the moment our lives changed, never to be changed back. Once children trade the innocence of childhood for the brutal reality and hard edge of life, there are no buybacks. The abuse became a familiar routine for me. Joseph and I never discussed it. No one did. We all just pretended it didn't happen and the world was happy to acquiesce. With no money, torn clothes, an empty refrigerator, and a prison of an apartment, I turned to the world of comic books to escape. I read every one I could get my hands on and had dreams only a child could have, dreams of the super strength to be able to stand up to Mike and not be afraid. The super strength never materialized, and the damage to my childhood was irreparable.

After years of this painful monotony, my grandmother loaned my mother some money to buy a small house just up the road in Liberty Park, Queens. Although it was a short walk from the apartment over the bar, it was miles away in terms of an environment for raising a child. Now on and off with her relationship with Mike, my mother began to work for Con Edison, a New York electricity provider, and earned a better salary. Some of the hardest edges to our lives began to soften, but Mike's edge was as sharp as ever. After a night of drinking he managed to get to our house and began banging on the windows. The relentless banging terrified me and my brothers and we braced for the repercussions if the window gave and he got ahold of us. The only thing Mike ever appeared to fear was the police, so I quickly dialed 911 and counted the seconds until they arrived. I remember watching them at our front door after they ordered Mike to leave and knowing, at that moment, that I wanted to be one of them. I wanted to be able to pay back the favor and bring peace to a young child's life.

2

NYPD BLUE

EARLY CHILDHOOD EXPERIENCES instilled in me a deep desire to never be physically intimidated again, and to do everything in my limited power to ensure it did not happen to others. Law enforcement became a dream of mine, and after two years of college I began to research careers in federal, state, and local law enforcement. After making a number of calls to the FBI, DEA, US Marshals, and Secret Service, I realized that I was up against steep competition for the limited number of entry-level positions available and that moving from college directly into a law-enforcement position with one of these agencies was going to be dif-

ficult if not impossible. I began to consider different paths and after careful
consideration settled on the New York City Police Department as the best
organization to acquire both the experience and the contacts necessary to
move into federal law enforcement. I decided on the NYPD cadet program
as the most logical choice, and my father was eager to help.

My father had always dreamed of a career in law enforcement, but
a severe case of scoliosis of the spine had prevented him from following
through on those dreams. The cadet program was, in essence, a paid intern-
ship program. It allowed me to attend college full time while working
part time for the department in a support capacity, with a contract that
obligated me to two years of service as a police officer upon graduation.
The program was an initiative by the NYPD to recruit more college
graduates into their ranks and in a short time it attracted a number of
well-qualified applicants.

At this same period in my life I was considering military service as
well and was in touch with a recruiter for the US Marine Corps. Staff
Sergeant Williams and I engaged in a number of conversations and my
desire to serve our country was strong. My uncle, Gregory Ambrose, was
killed in action in Vietnam and my mother never recovered from this
tragedy. I knew she would be traumatized by my decision if I entered into
military service, but the calling was loud and strong. I vividly recall my
high school's job fair and attending the Marine Corps presentation and
being magnetically drawn to the heroism the presiding Marine appeared
to exude from every pore.

Despite the gravitational pull of military service on me, unfortunately,
I would never fulfill my desire to serve, a decision I would question for
many years afterward. I received a phone call months after submitting
my application to the NYPD telling me I had successfully completed the
rigorous application process for the cadet program and had to report for
duty in the spring of 1995. At the time, I was living on my own and struggling financially. I moved out of my house after a physical altercation with
Mike shortly after my eighteenth birthday and was working and attending
college while trying to figure out my future. Financial pressures weighed
on me daily and I knew if I took the cadet position military service would
not be an option, but it would give me some financial stability and a path
forward. My law-enforcement dreams and my desire to escape perpetual

financial pressure led me to accept the position. My mother cried with relief when I told her the news and the thought of losing another member of her family subsided.

I was excited to join the NYPD cadet program. It was my first real job that involved mature responsibilities and I was honored to be a part of the program. Although the job required maturity, I was still just a city kid with a rough edge and was unfamiliar with the formality of a paramilitary environment. The cadet training program was a mini police academy run by officers with strong military backgrounds. The paramilitary atmosphere began on the first day when I reported for duty at a local college auditorium, I had barely made it to the line to access the facility when a grizzled NYPD veteran screamed, "Get in line, and shut your mouths!" That was all I needed to hear to fully comprehend that my life was about to change.

Upon graduating from the cadet training program and becoming well-versed in military marching, the law, and most importantly the law-enforcement culture, I was assigned to the 114th Precinct in Astoria, Queens. After an awkward few days wandering around the precinct aimlessly waiting for my shift to end, I was asked by precinct supervisors to see if I could help "upstairs." The second floor of the 114th Precinct was known as "the borough," or the command center for the entire borough of Queens. The top NYPD brass from Queens worked upstairs along with the staff they imported from precincts around the city. It was no place for a cadet, the lowest-ranking uniformed member in the department, and I didn't exactly get off on the right foot. On my first full day at the borough I was assigned to an afternoon shift after my college classes ended. When I arrived, I dutifully signed in the log that I was beginning my shift. Ten minutes later I found out that I had committed the mortal sin of signing in at the actual time I had arrived and "blocked out" a chief who arrived late and was now obligated to sign in at her actual (late) arrival time. I was not off to the best start, but after serving a penance of performing menial tasks and a period of public humiliation by the borough staff, I was forgiven.

Given my young appearance, it was not long before an affable sergeant who had taken a liking to me asked me if I would be interested in doing undercover work. Sergeant Schwach asked me if I could report to the 111th Precinct in Bayside, Queens, to accompany a team on alcohol enforcement operations. I was not a police officer yet and did not carry a weapon but the assignment appeared benign enough. Bayside was a popular middle-class Queens neighborhood with a vibrant bar section (coincidentally where I would later meet my wife). The bars brought economic activity to the area but also significant crime and trouble from underage drinkers and irresponsible patrons. Some of the local delis and convenience stores contributed to the problem by selling alcohol to underage customers. My task was to accompany a small unit of police officers and a sergeant and attempt to purchase alcohol from the stores and bars. The brief ride to the first bar on the Long Island Expressway service road was an experiment in emotional suppression. I did not want the officers to realize how nervous I was, so I engaged in small talk to cover my anxiety as we drove over to the Pull-Box.

The Pull-Box was a local bar owned by a former New York fireman (a fact, I was to discover later, that played into the decision to include it in the undercover operation). I walked into the bar feigning bravery and sat down among a crowd of fewer than five patrons, which only drew more attention to my awkward entry, and asked for a beer. When the bartender asked me for an ID, I responded that I didn't have one and he asked me to leave. I was relieved that he did the right thing since I was completely unprepared as to what to do if he actually served me the beer. When I reappeared, the look of disappointment on the officers' faces was clear. I found out later that one of them had a grudge against the bar owner. It was my first exposure to the rough underbelly of law enforcement.

After a number of weeks acting as an undercover and making underage alcohol purchases, I became comfortable with the process and the under-cover work became second nature. It was a skill I would use later as a Secret Service agent. The process was clean and efficient: walk in, grab a beer, pay for it, pretend I forgot something, and walk out. The officers would then rush in and write the owner a criminal court summons. I performed my role well enough to be considered for reassignment to a new unit in the borough that was to focus on serial criminals, a line of work I found incredibly interesting given my academic background in psychology The unit was called the Pattern Identification Module and its mission was to analyze data on major crimes and attempt to uncover patterns that could be relayed to detective teams for use in their investigations. My job was to input and analyze data, often for hours at a time. In one case, I began to notice a series of serial home-invasion–type robberies where the criminal would say the same thing each time he would knock on a door of a home he intended to break into.

This early success in detecting patterns in the serial robbery cases allowed me a degree of workplace freedom I was not used to in my short time with the NYPD. This gave me credibility with the officers and the sergeant I worked for, and they subsequently allowed me to make my own hours. With the new, flexible work schedule and the companionship of a good team, I enjoyed this assignment immensely and spent the next two years working with the team.

After a few months working in the program, I became friends with a fellow cadet in the program named Marty (who, ironically, I later reconnected with after he saw one of my appearances on *Wilkow* on TheBlaze TV). During our commutes back to the police academy in Manhattan for ongoing training, Marty liked to talk about politics and was the first person to introduce me to the ideological principles of conservatism. Although I was always passionate about economics and politics, my understanding at the time was limited and my larger perspective was lacking. Our long, sometimes confrontational conversations triggered my interest into why the big questions never seemed to be answered. Why were there pockets of poverty despite decades of antipoverty programs? Why did universal health care really equate to excellent health care for some and universal mediocrity for others? Why did some schools excel yet others fail miserably despite access being guaranteed? Marty did not know it at the time but he sparked an interest that would alter my life permanently.

As my graduation from college approached and my time as a police cadet came to a close, I began to prepare for the next stage of my career with the NYPD. My contractual obligation to serve for two years as a police officer upon graduation from college was about to start, and I looked forward to the opportunity. The cadet program was an interesting experience because I learned about the organizational structures and psychology of law enforcement from the inside. The culture of law enforcement is unique in its clear divide between those who carry the guns and those who do not, regardless of their background or qualifications. Entering the police academy in the summer of 1997, now for the second time, was an easier transition compared to the cultural shift I experienced entering the cadet program as a teenager. I found the training to be somewhat redundant and spent the majority of my time building relationships with other classmates.

After nearly nine months of academy training, we were ready to pick our "wish list" of precinct assignments before being assigned to an FTU, or "Field Training Unit." My FTU, where I would spend one month, was the 32nd Precinct in Harlem, a challenging assignment for a new officer. However, I selected the most difficult precinct within the NYPD borders for my first permanent assignment, the 75th Precinct in East New York, Brooklyn. I chose this notoriously dangerous precinct for two reasons, the primary reason being that I knew the assignment would be difficult and I relished the challenge, the secondary reason being that I knew I would be granted my wish, since no one actually requested the 75th.

Field training was the pinnacle of the police academy experience and a welcome break from the monotony of the classroom and regimented nature of the academy environment. The standard-issue NYPD uniform was dark blue, but while in field training we were permitted to wear only our gray police academy uniform. We were "rookies" to the police officers and residents of the precinct. Standing at my first roll call hearing the chant of "rookies, rookies" was slightly humiliating, yet funny. It was not funny later on when nearly everyone who passed me on my foot post made similar comments. I quickly learned that no matter the outside temperature, it was always wise to bring your standard-issue NYPD jacket, the same one worn by every other police officer, and cover up your gray shirt.

The gray shirts acted as a "scarlet letter" and forced the recruit class to bond together. I found companionship in the other recruits assigned to the 32nd Precinct with me, many of whom I had never met before. A fellow recruit named Brian was assigned to partner with me on our nightly foot patrols and we became fast friends. New York is a large city by population but is made relatively small by networks of friends and families, and, Brian's cousin was a friend of my brother's and we knew some of the same people. We spent hours talking while walking our assigned foot post, and, as I would learn throughout my law-enforcement career, things could change in an instant. We would move from a conversation about baseball and the neighborhood to a foot pursuit through upper Manhattan and back to a conversation about a neighborhood friend. Brian and I would remain lifelong friends as a result of these foot patrol conversations, and our children would later grow up together.

Most of the police officers treated us as a precinct sideshow and largely ignored us, but after a few days some of them warmed to us. This would change rapidly for me one weekday afternoon.

I was walking my assigned foot post and as I turned a corner I saw a man seated on a store railing smoking what appeared to be marijuana. I was excited yet apprehensive, as this was the first police action I was about to engage in. As I slowly approached him he jumped down and began to run. I screamed into my radio "10-85," which was the nonemergency call for assistance, and immediately heard the cacophony of sirens as seemingly every police car in the precinct activated them at the same time. I chased him for a long city block until he was cut off by an assisting officer in a car and placed in handcuffs. Feeling relieved, I transported the man back to the precinct with the assisting officers who, rather than congratulating me, proceeded to lecture me on wasting police assets on "weed." The stern lecture from the sergeant on duty at the precinct was even more emotionally devastating, but it did teach me a lesson that would become a staple of my political philosophy. It taught me that there are real consequences to having an unreasonably idealistic view of the world.

In a perfect world, recreational drugs such as marijuana would exist strictly for ethical uses such as medical treatment. But the world is not perfect; it is a place where legislative decisions and law making involve trade-offs with very real consequences. Getting into a foot pursuit with a man who was smoking marijuana in public may seem like the right thing to do in a black-and-white world. In the real world, however, it involves police officers putting their lives at risk driving at high speeds and then removal of numerous police personnel from the streets to help in the administrative portion of the arrest. Another devastating consequence is the untold damage of an arrest for what even the most ardent law advocates among us would call a minor offense. With the perpetuity of the Internet and the permanent scar of a criminal record, this man's life has been altered permanently. The costs far outweigh the benefits.

Field training ended with a quick good-bye to the precinct personnel and an order to report back to the police academy the following week for graduation. Graduation ceremonies in the NYPD are a sight to behold. The event takes place at Madison Square Garden, and thousands of graduating recruits gather with their friends and families to celebrate the occasion. It was the last time I would see a number of my fellow recruits from the academy as we moved on to our careers with the department. Officer Stacie Williamson, a member of my training class, was shot and killed not long after graduation, and Officer Daniel O'Sullivan was struck by a vehicle while rendering aid to a stranded motorist and never physically or psychologically recovered, sad reminders of the daily perils of putting a badge on your chest and a gun on your hip.

My permanent assignment to the 75th Precinct began with the same rookie hazing rituals I was already accustomed to from both the academy and field training. But the hazing process in the 75th was much harsher than the one we experienced in the FTU. The police officers in the 75th were a street-hardened group. This Brooklyn precinct had a citywide reputation for being the toughest place to work given its consistently high crime rate and as a hiding spot for problem officers. Most of East New York, from the Belt Parkway to the entrance to Cypress Hills Street, was part of the 75th. This area was a world away from Manhattan, the financial capital of the world, and even the gentrified areas of Brooklyn could not have been more different. It was consistently scarred by drug wars, gang wars, racial intolerance, and urban blight. It was sad to watch, and as I began my assignment with daily foot patrols in the toughest areas of the precinct, I witnessed, up close and personal, the real human cost of social policy most politicians and bureaucrats only read about in books. The devastation was nothing short of tragic: generational poverty and dependence the likes of which are frequently unseen in a country as prosperous as ours. The lives of the neighborhood residents were ignored by the media, politicians, and bureaucrats until something was needed from them: votes, sound bites for the evening newscast while covering another crime scene, or a backdrop for another politician's vapid speech about a new piece of legislation he was sponsoring.

Eight hours a day, five to seven days a week, I would walk alone in the neighborhood from six at night until two o'clock in the morning, thinking about and digesting everything around me. It was emotionally devastating to see the hopelessness in the eyes of the residents of the neighborhood. One interaction stands out to me as an illustration of the difference between our "American Dream" and the dreams of a child I met while on patrol.

It was late at night, approximately eleven o'clock, and I was walking my typical patrol route when I noticed a child on a street corner known to be a hangout for drug dealers and prostitutes. The boy could not have been older than eight, yet he seemed very comfortable in his surroundings. I started up a conversation and asked him where he lived. He pointed across the street to one of the 75th Precinct's numerous housing projects and said, "There." I asked him about his parents and he proceeded to tell me that they let him stay out "late." As I walked him back to his building I asked him the typical questions any adult would ask a young child:

"What do you want to do when you grow up?"

He said, "I dunno, but I want to be like AZ."

I had a hard time hearing him and thought he had said he wanted to be like Jay-Z, who at that time was a young, up-and-coming rapper. I said, "Jay-Z?"

The child responded, "No, AZ!"

He then handed me a flyer from his pocket about a local neighborhood kid using the name AZ who would perform on a nearby corner in a few days. I asked him if he had any other plans, to which he responded, "Whatta you mean?"

I walked him across the street and watched him go into the building, but I never forgot that interaction. It left a scar on me that has not healed. I asked myself over and over, why was this boy left out? I wondered why being a doctor, accountant, engineer, soldier, or anything else most children at some time think about was not an option for this child? Why was his future seemingly predetermined, while mine was an open book? Why did legions of politicians and bureaucrats feign interest in the plight of decent people living in the area yet ignore them when the results they promised never materialized? I would never let these questions go.

3

IN THE LINE OF FIRE

BEING A POLICE OFFICER in New York City is like no other job in the world. Things change quickly. The shift from extreme boredom to adrenaline-inducing danger can happen in seconds. I was very conscious of the fact that working the most dangerous shift in the precinct with the highest crime rate in New York City could alter my plans to join a federal law-enforcement agency, or any other line of employment, very quickly. This was never more evident than during a foot patrol on Fulton Street in the winter of 1998.

It was after midnight and I was fatigued from the cold weather and the long day I had had before even reporting for work. The streets were surprisingly quiet that night, likely due to the cold weather. With no one to talk to for hours and all the shutters on the storefronts closed, the night seemed endless. This all changed in an instant when the silence was broken by my handheld radio: "GLA Central, in pursuit, slowly!" A GLA was a grand larceny auto, a stolen car, and the officer was in pursuit. Central was the name we used for the dispatcher, and the officer was sure to mention he was pursuing "slowly." All officers said this because high-speed vehicle pursuits were strictly forbidden unless under emergency circumstances, and vehicle theft did not qualify. If they failed to mention it was a "slow" pursuit, even if it wasn't, the duty sergeant would order it halted.

As the officer in pursuit began to describe his route, "northbound toward Fulton," I realized that they were quickly headed in my direction. The next thing I saw was a set of headlights, followed by an incredibly loud crash. The thief had driven the stolen car right through the metal shutters on a storefront and the vehicle was lodged halfway inside the store. I ran to assist with my heart pounding and was the first to get inside the store. The thief exited the car and was attempting to escape when I tackled him and briefly held him while the other officers arrived. These types of experiences were all too common in the 75th.

As my time in the 75th Precinct wore on, I began to grow impatient with the glacial pace of the application process for the federal law-enforcement positions. Attending graduate school full time at the City University of New York and dealing with nightly adrenaline dumps with the NYPD was wearing me down. By this time, I had narrowed my choices down to three federal agencies: the FBI (my preference), the DEA, and the US Secret Service.

After submitting the voluminous paperwork, by chance one day I struck up a conversation with a woman in my local gym while running a treadmill. She was an NYPD detective who happened to work with a task force unit in which one of the members was a Secret Service agent. She proceeded to extol the virtues of the Secret Service and sing the praises of the agent. She was completely unaware of the fact that with that brief interaction, she had altered my life. I began to vigorously pursue my progress in the application process with the Secret Service, to the point where the administrative assistant assigned to the New York field office recruitment section knew me by first name. My staying active in the process surely annoyed the recruitment section staff, but it moved the process along rapidly. I took the written examination, reported to the field office for an interview with a panel of agents, had a follow-up interview, received a thorough medical examination, and suffered through the necessary indignity of a full-scope polygraph examination all in the period of approximately six months.

The polygraph test is an experience every agent recalls with horror. It is an eight-hour interrogation designed to break even the most skilled subject. Mine was no different. I was grilled with such questions as, "Have you ever lied to your parents?" and "Have you ever cheated on a test?" There is never any indication if you passed or failed, and after the misery of the test has concluded you wait for days and sometimes weeks for an answer as to your status. I received the call approximately two weeks after completing the polygraph test from an agent named Madeline who, to my immeasurable relief, said, "Congratulations, you are moving on."

The polygraph test was the drop-out point for most applicants to the Secret Service. Many did not pass and I knew that since I did, my chances of being hired were very good. It was the last step in the rigorous process and now I could only wait for a hiring decision. The waiting period was filled with anxiety because I desperately needed a change of scenery. Attending graduate school full time while working full time as a police officer was strenuous, and allocating time for studying was difficult. I frequently volunteered to work in the precinct holding cells, an assignment virtually no one wanted, because it gave me brief periods to read school material.

Working in the cells in a precinct with an exceptionally high crime rate was tough. It was not uncommon to be berated by the inmates for the entire eight-hour shift. I would occasionally laugh at the creativity of some of those arrested. Standard insults were usually not good enough, and all the prisoners could hear each other so it became a competition to determine who could say the most deranged things to the officer in the cells. I learned to develop a thick skin, which would serve me well in the political arena later. After weeks of this, I desperately wanted out and prayed nightly for that final phone call from the Secret Service. That phone call came in May of 1999.

I was in the cells listening to the nightly cacophony of insults when a "house mouse" (a precinct officer who has never worked the streets) walked into the cells and said, "Bongino, phone call in the CAPS room."

I walked inside, picked up the phone, and heard my recruiter, Madeline, say, "Congratulations, Dan, your reporting date is going to be June 21."

Although I expected the call, it was still an incredible feeling of achievement to be accepted by this elite agency. The officers in the room congratulated me and I walked back into the cells knowing I had accomplished something special. I called my mother and father to let them know that my journey from that frightened child rescued by the police to the elite ranks of the US Secret Service was complete, and for the remainder of that day the prisoners' taunts sounded like choir music.

I reported for my first day as an employee of the Secret Service on June 21, 1999. I took the subway to the World Trade Center station and proudly ascended the escalator into the plaza ready to tackle this new phase of my life. I sat in the lobby of the Secret Service's flagship New York office with three other new hires—Lisa, Don, and Tom—waiting to be summoned into the inner sanctum of the field office where only Secret Service employees were allowed. When the door opened, our new supervisor, Tim, welcomed us and we began the long indoctrination process into the Secret Service culture.

Tim was a loud and sometimes obnoxious man, but on protection assignments these are traits that can serve an agent well. His large frame and booming voice contributed to what was to some an imposing presence. We spent the first month working under Tim's supervision, with little to do other than fill out administrative paperwork, serve as the butt of Tim's politically incorrect humor, and assist the other agents in the office. We were not authorized to carry weapons yet or to serve in any type of law-enforcement capacity, so we were idle waiting for a new trainee class to begin at the Federal Law Enforcement Training Center (FLETC) in Brunswick, Georgia. When the official notification from Secret Service headquarters arrived that we would begin training at FLETC in July of 1999, we felt relief that our next step was confirmed. The relief was short-lived, however, as the agents in the office informed us that temperatures in Brunswick, Georgia, hovered in the high nineties for most of July and August.

Tom and I decided we were going to drive to FLETC, and I followed

him for the entire fifteen-hour journey. Tom had worked in the financial
services field before joining the Secret Service and we remained friends
throughout our careers. Tom sought out a career in the Secret Service
for the same general reason I did: a desire to do something bigger than
the offerings life had currently placed in front of him. I found his humor,
sometimes at my expense, to be a calming influence in the high-stress
environment of the Secret Service. Being able to stay calm under intense
stress is an invaluable skill within the Secret Service, and many of the
men and women within the agency, like Tom, used humor to break the
tension on dangerous assignments.

Tom and I arrived at the facility close to midnight and were sent to
our quarters, a dilapidated series of dorms affectionately known as the
"Crack Houses." Needless to say, the dorms were old and the upkeep
was sadly lacking. Despite the harsh name, I didn't mind the housing
arrangement. I lived as a child in far worse conditions, and not having to
pay rent was refreshing.

We met the rest of our Secret Service training class the next day. These
twenty-four men and women would be my companions and coworkers
for the majority of the next nine months. It was an impressive group, with
personalities bound to clash for all the right reasons. Everyone fit the psy-
chological profile for type A classification. Our group included Sue, the
biochemist and outspoken perfectionist; Reggie, the strong, silent type
who was always digesting his surroundings; Mike, the class clown but loyal
friend to those loyal to him; and Chris, the former college football player
who was the voice of reason when excitement overtook common sense.

The classroom portion of the training was standard: law, investigative
tactics, crime scene processing, and other courses designed to make us
experts in the art of catching criminals. Practical exercises were the bread
and butter of the training and a welcome respite from the tedium of daily
lectures. The FLETC staff hired actors to play specific roles in a mock
criminal investigation, which was tied into all of the classroom work. It
was a brilliant training strategy, and the knowledge we needed to absorb
became very real to us as we simultaneously learned about federal criminal
investigations in the classroom and experienced one in the ongoing simula-
tion. The entire process was graded, and I was as competitive a personality
as could be found. I had a hard time in my quest to win the physical fitness

award due to the incredible collective fitness level of my class, but I fought
for the academic honor until the last test. Sue and I had a friendly rivalry
for the entire nine weeks and we would constantly ask each other, at the
end of each test, "What did you get?" To my disappointment, on the
final exam for the course, Sue outscored me by less than one half of one
point. She and I would compete for the rest of our careers and although
we never asked the question "What did you get?" again, we were always
looking over our shoulders at each other in a race to the top.

The final weeks of training were the easiest. The workload was lighter,
the Georgia heat began to relent, and a devastating back injury I sus-
tained in the initial days of training began to heal. I partially ruptured
two spinal disks taking a sit-up test and rather than accepting a "recycle"
(trainees who were injured were typically sent back to their originating
field offices to heal and would begin again in a new training class, referred
to as "recycles"), I soldiered through the program. This was a mistake I
would pay for dearly, as the injury never properly healed and would haunt
not only the rest of my Secret Service career, but my ability to physically
perform to the high standards I had set for myself.

Although, in the final weeks, our coursework was nearly over, the
training class's internal strife was not. We all got along rather well, but
living and working with the same group of people for nine consecutive
weeks with no break is bound to create conflict, both real and imagined.
There was a love triangle; a cheating allegation against one recruit who, it
was alleged, skipped a lap on the mile-and-a-half run test (cheating in the
Secret Service is a crime that is never forgiven); and occasional weekend
fights in bars from Saint Simons Island to Savannah. These conflicts were
real, although the imagined ones were far worse. It seemed that each day
someone would invent a new reason to be angry at a classmate deemed a
"slacker." The same few men and women quickly developed reputations for
laziness and apathy and the stories about them spread like raging wildfire.
As it turned out, some of those men and women would have problems
throughout their careers, and one of them was terminated shortly after
graduation for an off-duty altercation.

Graduation day, though eagerly anticipated, was anticlimactic. The
brief ceremony was held in the chapel on the FLETC grounds, but we still
had another eleven-week training course to complete at the Secret Service

training center in Laurel, Maryland. Most of us were content to shake hands with a brief, "See you in Maryland." The eleven-week session was the second and final phase of our training, and the class was eager to get it started.

I was fascinated by each and every classroom course we took and was equally impressed with the agency's dedication to marksmanship and skill with firearms. Handling a firearm anywhere near the president of the United States is a solemn responsibility, and the Secret Service places a heavy premium on mastery of your firearm. We were scheduled for range time nearly every day of the course, and the instruction was rigorous and unlike anything I experienced at the New York police academy or FLETC.

Both the classroom and firearms instructors were knowledgeable, and all had fascinating stories to tell of traveling the world with presidents from Nixon to Clinton. During breaks in training we would crowd around and listen to their surreal tales. The instructors were all openly proud of their service and the agency that had become such an important part of their lives, and it carried over to the students. The Secret Service has a culture specific to it and it alone due to its incomparable dual mission of protection and multifaceted investigations. Embedding this culture within every student trainee is an important goal of every instructor, a fact I was to be reminded of repeatedly when I was to return as an instructor years later.

One instructor every agent in my training class remembered is Dan E. Dan later penned a piece about his time in the Secret Service and was as tough a human being as I had ever encountered. A former US Marine, he would not hesitate to kick sand in your face on the tough 200-yard obstacle course if he felt you were not giving it a 100 percent effort. He respected the hard workers but had no time for malingerers or excuse seekers. This made him a favorite target for management's ire, as they did not appreciate his candor. Ironically, as I began to comment publicly about the Secret Service over a decade later during my campaign for the US Senate, most of the media outlets that would ask for an interview would call either me or Dan, depending on who was available.

Explaining the course was always a bore when I would call home and tell friends about my daily schedule, but learning about the secrets buried in something as ordinary as a dollar bill was eye opening. We walked through the process of making money, spending time at a secret facility where the proprietary paper used to print our currency is made, then following the paper to the Bureau of Engraving and Printing in Washington, DC, to watch it turn into US currency. It was during this part of the training that I experienced the thrill of my first ride in an airplane. Growing up in a financially struggling family, air travel had never been an option for me.

Classes on credit card fraud were detailed and more complex than the other coursework. Stealing someone's credit card information was once a simple endeavor that has evolved into a technologically sophisticated criminal enterprise. When credit cards were first introduced to the US market, businesses would manually process them using paper carbon copies of the card. When these copies were thrown away, criminals saw an opportunity and the art of "Dumpster diving" evolved. Criminals would steal the carbon copy slips with the credit card numbers on them from the Dumpsters of businesses and then make fake credit cards with the stolen numbers. With the dawn of fully electronic processing, more sophisticated theft techniques emerged. We learned about "skimming," where the criminal takes your credit card during a transaction and swipes it through the business processor and then through his own device, which stores the information from the magnetic strip. The information from the magnetic strip is then electronically coded onto a new card.

In addition to the financial crimes courses, we were slowly introduced to the methods the Secret Service employs in its best-known responsibility: protecting the president. The AOP (assault on principal) training, where an actor playing the role of the president was subjected to various attack scenarios, was intense and could get painful. Each day was a new scenario where our unfortunate role player would be shot at, stabbed, punched, harassed, and generally manhandled for most of the simulations. The Secret Service prefers realism in its training environment and uses weapons that fire "Simunition" bullets. Simunition cartridges feature plastic bullets that are harder than traditional paintballs and contain a waxy, colored substance that lets others know you have been shot. You, on the other hand, know *immediately* when you have been shot with a Simunition round because it is extremely painful, and being hit in sensitive areas such as the hands is an experience you will not forget, especially in cold weather when the wax hardens. Training with these rounds teaches new agents to quickly get behind cover and not to be "cowboys."

During one particular exercise in the Secret Service tactical village, our protectee came under a full assault from some of the instructors. I remember being hit over and over, scrambling to find cover quickly. I managed to fit my six-foot, two-hundred-pound frame behind a fire hydrant on the street and fire back, hitting one of the instructors at least three times. He backed off, we managed to keep the "president" alive for the exercise, and I acquired a collection of twenty-plus deep purple welts as a reminder of my lesson that day.

Our training class was scheduled to graduate in December of 1999, and the tension in the law-enforcement community throughout the country was high. The fear of a worldwide computer network collapse in the Y2K scare engrossed the nation, and the threat of terrorism was growing exponentially. My class was anxious to graduate and get out in the field to work. Final exams and the final physical fitness test were on everyone's mind.

The physical fitness training in the Secret Service is intense, and five areas are tested in order to graduate: maximum sit-ups and push-ups in one minute, maximum chin-ups (no time limit), a flexibility test, and the one-and-a-half-mile run. I was desperate to receive a mark of "excellent" on all the components of the test and was well above the standards for my age in every one but the run, where I hovered just seconds above the required completion time for a score of "excellent" (ten minutes and sixteen seconds). In between studying for the final exams in protection, protection intelligence, and financial crimes, I ran at every opportunity.

I enjoyed my runs with Sean, a classmate and former military policeman, who was amusingly robotic in his approach to any task. He viewed any problem or task unemotionally and had earned the class's respect for his ability to stay calm and adapt to any obstacle thrown at us. I ran with him often because, despite the weather or our fatigue, he never complained, and this kept me focused.

I was anxious on the day of the final physical fitness test. I felt I could not leave the academy without excelling in every category, and the run was weighing heavily on me. The run was the last portion of the test that day and it was freezing and raining, which made it increasingly difficult to breathe. I exerted myself fully in the other components and nearly doubled the requirements for an excellent score, but I was tiring myself out. As

I began the run, my breathing was labored within the first quarter mile, yet I ran at a pace far exceeding my comfort zone. And I paid the price: the second and third quarter miles felt like running through wet concrete. My legs felt like anchors, but I was not going to graduate without the satisfaction of completing this goal. The last quarter mile was as painful an experience as I can remember, and I knew if I slowed down for even a step I would fall short of the required time. I gathered a final bit of stored energy and sprinted the last fifty yards to the finish line. The instructor yelled out ten-sixteen." The training experience ended on a high note.

4

THE END OF
THE CLINTON ERA

ALTHOUGH I BEGAN my Secret Service career in the New York field office, I was notified after graduating from the training program that I would be transferred to the Melville, New York, field office. The news was a disappointment; I planned on relocating back into the city I grew up in and working in the field office there. Tom was also the recipient of some unexpected news, as he was transferred to our office at John F. Kennedy International Airport in Queens.

Both Tom and I understood that the majority of the high-profile criminal investigations and protection assignments originated in the New

York City office, it being the Secret Service's flagship office. The Melville field office—located in Suffolk County, about thirty miles outside the city—had a reputation for being "slow." Some of my New York agent friends called it the "Melville Country Club." This reputation quickly changed in September of 1999 when then President Bill Clinton and his wife, Hillary, purchased a home in the sleepy Westchester town of Chappaqua, New York. Rumors soon swirled that the first lady would seek the United States Senate seat of a New York icon, retiring Senator Daniel Patrick Moynihan.

The agent in charge of the Melville field office, Marty, was a "by the book" manager. He was a deeply religious and principled man who supported his men and the Secret Service mission with vigor and a sense of duty. When Marty heard of the Clinton's purchase of the Chappaqua home, he knew a firestorm was headed his way. A run for the US Senate by the wife of the sitting president of the United States would have been a protective workload of enormous consequence for the agents and management of the New York field office, but they had the personnel to support it. The Melville field office had only nine agents. We simply did not have the manpower to support frequent campaign visits by Mrs. Clinton, and on top of that, most of the agents in the office had fewer than two years of Secret Service protection experience. A visit by the first lady was an incredibly detailed and elaborate operation that was typically left to veteran agents who had experience with the Presidential Protective Division (PPD).

The PPD was psychologically intense, and the agents in it typically had a minimum of seven years of experience and were hand-selected as the best of the best. They had no tolerance for rookie agents with no experience in "the big show" (a term some PPD agents would use for presidential protection). To further complicate an already-difficult operational requirement, there was no historical precedent for this. No current first lady had ever run for office before, and any protection model would have to be created with complex political concerns in mind.

Security is not as simple as placing a protectee in a bulletproof glass box. Security plans must be designed to guarantee a degree of protection while still allowing access to the principal. When that principal is a candidate for political office, it adds necessary layers of access not required of other protectees, because the fear of losing an election makes both candidates and their staff act in strange ways.

I could see from our initial meeting with Scott, a polished and well-respected PPD agent assigned to the first lady, that this assignment was going to require an "on-the-job" training component that was nothing resembling the traditional program the Secret Service implemented for its new agents. I was going to have to learn quickly how to use my knowledge from the classroom in real, high-stakes situations, and the consequences of failure were unthinkable. Reputation management in the Secret Service is a skill you must learn quickly. Complaining about work conditions is frowned upon, and the peer pressure on those who choose to violate this credo is oppressive. Dealing with the PPD this early in my career could have been a great opportunity, or it could have been the end of my career. If I excelled, I would have done so in the eyes of fellow agents who, due to their seniority and prestigious position on the PPD, would likely have been my supervisors in the near future. But if I failed, it would have done the kind of damage that could not have been undone. There were also considerations in dealing with the numerous local police departments in Long Island's Nassau and Suffolk counties. Their cooperation was paramount to our success. They all had their own ideas of how to properly secure perimeters and conduct motorcades, and I quickly learned how to conduct domestic diplomacy among our law-enforcement partners.

I was both excited and humbled to be embedded in the Clinton campaign and on the front lines of what was to become the most expensive Senate campaign in US history. Not a week passed without a notification from PPD operations in Washington that we should expect a visit from the first lady, and days off were nonexistent. She was not polling well on Long Island and although she did not need to win the two Long Island counties, it was important that she perform well there. The political drama surrounding the campaign was intense and the campaign quickly turned into a national referendum on the Clintons.

Clinton's original opponent, former New York City mayor Rudy Giuliani, dropped his bid for the seat early in the summer of 2000, yet her campaign still faced challenges. Charges of "carpetbagger" (oddly enough a weak charge that would be leveled at me in my run for the US Senate in 2012) were constant, but watching the Clinton machine in action from behind the scenes was a like a PhD-level course in campaign management. Even seemingly innocuous issues became front-page stories. The campaign's selection of a vehicle, typically a nonissue in both the Secret Service and the press, became a story when they selected a two-tone brown Ford conversion van, which was far different from the fleet of black limousines the president and his family typically use. Within the Secret Service, the vehicle became affectionately known as "Scooby-Doo" due to its brown color. Looking back on the decision to select that dull brown van, I view it as a stroke of political genius. Every news outlet photo of Mrs. Clinton's arrivals was of her exiting this rather middle-class-looking van. This stuck with me years later during my own run for office, and I would constantly tell my team that campaigns are about "sound bites and snapshots." Short quotes and pictures tell a story to a busy collection of voters that long speeches can never do.

The Clintons had a close inner circle and wanted everything done their way, with few exceptions. This being my first political campaign on the "inside," I was initially disturbed at the level of sycophantic behavior from elected officials desperate to be associated with a winner. Whenever the Clinton staff would publicly release her plans to be on Long Island, the phone calls to Marty would begin. Every locally elected official on the Democratic side of the political fence would call looking for access, which Marty had no intention of granting, and when Mrs. Clinton arrived they would all line up like schoolchildren desperate to appear in a picture that would run in the newspaper. Observing this on a weekly basis left a stain in my heart regarding the true motivations of those who sought public office, one that has yet to be washed away.

When Long Island congressional representative Rick Lazio became the likely Republican nominee, replacing Rudy Giuliani, the pressure to salvage votes on Long Island became that much more intense for the Clinton campaign. In addition to the increasing number of visits to the area controlled by our small Secret Service office, the pressure of dealing with the local police became an issue.

Security is an art form, not a science, and for both practical and political reasons, the campaign did not want to burden all the local police assets each time they visited the area. The Clinton team did not want to drain the local police budgets, and the ever-present issue of the candidate appearing "accessible" created a number of uncomfortable moments in my dealings with the police. Although protection service was difficult, being part of the constant excitement surrounding a high-profile protectee was something the local police officers enjoyed, and the overtime pay only reinforced their tendency to want to be there when the first lady was in town. Asking the police to stand down when the security was sufficient to not require additional assets was a tough task. They genuinely wanted to help, and having been a uniformed police officer myself, I understood their position.

The campaign grew more difficult as we closed in on Election Day in November. The pressure to win was intense. A loss would tarnish the Clinton name and end a potential second legacy before it could begin. The tension was especially evident among the staff. I found the staff to be complete political opposites from my conservative leanings, but they were dedicated, loyal supporters of their cause and I quietly admired that.

My admiration for their dedication aside, we clashed frequently during the last few months of the campaign. Their job is to get their candidate elected and, although security is a concern for them, our methods are often misunderstood. Secret Service agents are responsible for reading over intelligence reports, speaking with the local police, and using their experience and training to put together a security plan with respect for the protectee's needs. The staff seemed to think some of our methods were unnecessary, and the battles became tiresome. I received a stern reprimand from Marty for one particular method I thought was a clever way to solve a security issue we were having at a local university.

I was assigned to secure an indoor speech site for Mrs. Clinton on a university campus and I noticed immediately that there was an adjacent building with windows that had a direct line of sight to the stage. Life as a Secret Service agent teaches you to quickly look at everything as a potential problem. If a gunman were to be stationed in one of those rooms he would be well within rifle range, and that concerned me greatly. I did not have enough security personnel between the campus police and the Secret Service agents to station someone in that building, so I had to devise a creative solution.

After a few hours of walking through the site with the problem churning in my mind, I had a eureka moment. I thought: fake snow.

I had remembered my mother painting our windows in the apartment above the bar with sprayed-on fake snow. I asked the host from the university if he wouldn't mind purchasing some cans of fake snow and spraying the windows to block the line of sight from the building. She agreed and did not appear bothered in any way by my request. On the day of the visit I patiently waited in front of the scheduled arrival area for the motorcade to arrive, always the most anxiety-ridden part of a visit. I said a short prayer hoping for the best, as I always did, and the motorcade approached and stopped on the exact spot we had rehearsed. I led the swarm of agents, staffers, host committee members and local politicians into the room and as I looked up at the windows, I saw to my dismay that they had a black coating that did not in any way resemble the fake snow we discussed. Putting this information aside, I focused on the rest of the visit, listened to Mrs. Clinton's remarks, guided her through an uneventful rope line full of excited students, and led her back to the car.

Proud of my work for the visit, I thanked everyone and gathered my equipment and left. It wasn't until the next day that I realized I had caused a stir on the campus. In lieu of fake snow, the university had purchased black spray paint and painted the windows with it. The university maintenance staff had tried desperately to remove it but was having a difficult time. The university staff then called Marty to thank him for the cooperation and mentioned the paint. Marty was upset about it and let me know immediately. I learned that day that when the Secret Service requests something, it was going to get done, but it was my responsibility to ensure it was done without undue burden. I apologized to the university and carried that lesson with me.

On election night of 2000 my campaign experience with the Clintons was coming to a close. It was bittersweet. I not only learned valuable lessons about our methodologies from the PPD agents assigned to the first lady, I also learned a lot about myself. I pushed myself harder than I ever had in my life and had come through it unscathed. After all the visits, motorcades, travels, and threats, Mrs. Clinton was alive and well, with not even a close call during the campaign.

But there was no rest for our weary bodies on election night, as the Melville field office was assigned to work the Hyatt in New York City, where Mrs. Clinton, her staff, and crowd of supporters would gather to monitor the returns. Personally I hoped for a national Republican victory that night, and held out hope that the party could also take the New York Senate seat.

Although I would have forfeited my life proudly for Mrs. Clinton in my role as a Secret Service agent, I was still a Republican and knew the party needed a win both nationally and in New York. That night I was receiving minute-by-minute updates on all the ongoing races from the Clinton staff, who the whole time were feigning disinterest in order to not create a scene in the event Mrs. Clinton lost. Adding to the chaos of the night, our hand-held metal detector failed at the checkpoint I was manning, and I was forced to have to manually pat down incoming guests. My first victim happened to be actor Ben Affleck, who was good-hearted about it.

As the night wore on and exit poll results came in, it became apparent that the first lady would be declared the winner. When the race was called for Mrs. Clinton it seemed like the entire hotel shook in elation. I was politically disappointed but touched by the outpouring of genuine emotion from the campaign staff I had come to know well. It was clear that they believed in their cause as passionately as I believed in mine. But the presidential election was an entirely different story.

I was relieved by another agent late that night and headed to my room still unclear as to who the next president was going to be, Texas governor George W. Bush or Vice President Al Gore. This decision had potent ramifications for me both politically and personally. The Clinton staff was confidently telling me that Gore "had it," but some of the skeptical ones were quietly saying that it was "not over." When Florida was declared for Gore by some media outlets, I was devastated. I felt that the obituary for the Republican Party had just been written.

I awoke the following day thinking that the first lady had won her race for New York's Senate seat and that our new president was Al Gore. To my astonishment when I turned on the television cable news channel, Florida was back in the "undecided" column. What followed was nearly a month of speculation and well-documented political theater, which had very real consequences for the Secret Service. With no margin for error in their planning, the Secret Service was forced to plan for a presidential security footprint for two presidents-elect, George W. Bush and Al Gore.

Planning for one presidential transition is difficult enough, within both the White House and the Secret Service, but planning for two was a situation that had never been considered. The chaos ended in mid-December 2000 when the Supreme Court halted the recount of the presidential ballots and George W. Bush was declared the winner.

5

9/11

SEPTEMBER 11, 2001, was a quiet, calm morning in our Long Island office. Tony, Joe, and I were planning a search warrant and arrest for an Internet fraudster who was "selling" diamonds on eBay (without the actual diamonds). While discussing the arrest logistics of the operation, Tom, a senior agent within the office who had developed a reputation for calm and who loved to say, "Take it easy" every time he felt an agent was getting emotional, rushed into my office shouting, "Someone just bombed the World Trade Center." He had been on the phone with our New York office located in 7 World Trade Center as the first plane struck the North Tower, and the New York dispatcher he was speaking to believed it to be a bomb.

Collectively stunned that the World Trade Center had been attacked again (Muslim terrorists had detonated a truck bomb in its underground garage in 1993), we dropped our arrest paperwork and rushed into the rear of the office where Marty had a cable news channel on . . . and nothing. There was no mention of any bomb at the World Trade Center. Marty began to change the channels and I remember as he stopped at the show *The View* he looked up and said, "I don't see anything."

At that point, we saw the dreaded "Breaking News" scroll across the screen and a live newscaster interrupt the program, clearly unprepared for what he was about to say. I don't recall any of his words or the words of anyone else in the room at that time, as I was transfixed on the television screen. There was a live image of a gaping hole in the side of the North Tower of the World Trade Center that appeared surreal. I had just been with some Secret Service friends at the Windows on the World restaurant on the top floors of the North Tower the week prior and had been marveling at the incredible 360-degree views. I also began my career with Tom, Lisa, and Don in the lobby of our 7 World Trade Center New York field office, and I frequently reflected on the moment when I ascended the escalator into the World Trade Center plaza on the day I was hired. It was one of my proudest moments, and the plaza always brought back feelings of renewal and goodwill. So it was a surreal image to watch papers and pieces of the building fall into that plaza below. Marty, who rarely showed any emotion and had chastised me many times during my time working for him for wearing my emotions on my sleeve, was clearly as shaken by the attack as the rest of us. His normally stoic face telegraphed the anger we were all feeling but not saying.

The news began reporting that a plane hit the building, and the first words I recall hearing were those of Paul, a new agent to the Melville office who had been a navigator in the US Navy with many hours in flight time, protesting, "There is no way in this weather a plane hit that tower." The sky was clear blue that morning and there was not a cloud in the sky.

We all watched, hypnotized by the tragedy. Although it was only seventeen minutes after the North Tower was struck that United Airlines Flight 175 struck the South Tower, it felt like days. We watched the second plane strike the South Tower in horror. I distinctly recall Marty saying "Holy shit!" as an incredible ball of fire screamed out of the opposite side of the tower. I knew, right at that moment, as most Americans did, that our definition of "normal" was about to be discarded. Life in America was now going to be defined in terms of pre-September 11 and post-September 11.

Any talk of the arrest we were planning was quickly forgotten and one of the longest, most emotionally devastating days of my life was just beginning. After quickly discussing with Marty the most effective way for us to help, we decided to drive to our satellite field office at JFK airport in Queens, where Tom was assigned, and begin the process of trying to locate the hundreds of Secret Service personnel who worked at the World Trade Center.

As we left, workers from the other businesses occupying the office building were walking aimlessly in the hallway crying and trying desperately to reach loved ones. The cell phone networks were overloaded, and completing an outgoing call was nearly impossible. The inability to complete a call was taking an emotional toll on me as I frantically attempted to reach my brother Joseph.

Joseph was an emergency medical technician with the New York City Fire Department, and knowing my brother, I was certain he had rushed to lower Manhattan to render aid. My cell phone rang as I opened the car door and I anxiously looked down hoping it was Joseph, but it was my father. I had never known him to be an outwardly emotional man, but he was crying on the phone, clearly with my brother in mind. It would be hours before I would hear from Joseph but regardless, we had to get to the JFK office to help.

At JFK we were met by Manny, a senior agent in the office, who told us that there were hundreds of agents unaccounted for and we should start paging them on their work-issued pagers and cross them off the list as they called into the office. As they called in one by one, they all told stories of unthinkable terror. They all mentioned the horror of witnessing terrified people in the towers who chose to jump rather than burn alive, and the sounds of bodies crashing against the pavement. I could never forget these stories and for years after when I would check into a high-rise hotel, I would look out the window and imagine the horror the victims of this attack felt when making the decision to jump.

There were also tales of heroism that emerged about the brave men and women of the Secret Service's New York field office who, rather than flee, stayed at the plaza to provide medical aid and assistance. Two agents, John and Tom, who despite multiple warnings ran into the North Tower to evacuate those who could not make it out under their own power, stand out to me as potent examples of the valor exhibited by many that tragic day. Both men were in the North Tower as the South Tower collapsed. They listened to the roar of the collapse and were blinded by dust and debris while trying to descend the North Tower's poorly lit stairwell. Lives were saved because of these two men, but it's something they rarely, if ever, discuss. Their heroism was the quiet type.

By the late afternoon of Tuesday, September 11, after crossing off name after name on my list of New York field office personnel who could be accounted for, only a few names remained on the list. With each passing minute our fear grew that their phone call would never come. We did not speak of their potential demise openly; we only guessed at possible reasons why they were not answering the pages we sent out. Finally, we received a call from an agent telling us the location of a large block of the missing agents, and we crossed off a swath of names. Some of the agents had evacuated people in boats and made it to New Jersey, but their pagers had fallen off, becoming casualties of the chaos.

Despite the relief that accompanied locating the agents, we still had two names remaining on the list. One was a friend of mine, Kevin, whom I worked with in the Melville office for a brief period. Kevin and Marty were not the best of friends during Kevin's time in Melville, but they learned to coexist. Kevin was a grizzled veteran who rarely withheld what he was thinking—the exact opposite of Marty, who was difficult to read. I had come to respect Kevin, and the thought of what had potentially happened to him was tough to bear. I was relieved when we received a call notifying us that he had been on assignment in Lagos, Nigeria, and was fine.

There was one name on that list that was never crossed off. As the evening hours approached, it was apparent that Craig Miller was going to be the only member of the Secret Service to never return home after the terrorist attacks. Master Special Officer Craig Miller perished on that fateful day, and given his history of service to this country in both the US Army and the Secret Service, it is thought that he died in the World Trade

Center plaza rendering medical aid to victims when the South Tower collapsed. Craig Miller died a hero in service to his country in a time of need.

Although the planes struck only the North and South Towers, the damage to the surrounding buildings after the collapse was substantial. The New York field office was located on the ninth floor of 7 World Trade Center. As the fires raged in the building it became structurally unsound and by 5:00 p.m. that day it collapsed, taking everything with it. All of the criminal case files, weapons, equipment, radios, armored vehicles, and agents' personal effects were gone. As I drove home that night from the JFK office, I made one final stop at the Melville office and saw Marty talking to an agent I knew from New York. The agent was coated in the now-infamous white dust from the collapse of the towers and was holding a bag with a Heckler & Koch MP5 submachine gun. I asked him why he had the MP5 and he responded, "It may be the only thing that made it out of the building."

In the days and weeks following the attacks, the pain and horror were compounded by the bitter feelings the special agents of the New York office felt regarding the Secret Service management's response. As the days passed and our detached leaders, who rarely left their insulated offices in our DC headquarters, did not visit the site of the attack, the anger grew into an open fury rarely seen in an agency proud of its culture of both discipline and secrecy. It was my first taste of the divide between the emotional response of the working-class Secret Service agents and the "cocktail party" managerial class's callous attitude. Bureaucracy spawns a lack of accountability, and that lack of accountability spawns an indifference that I would later come to learn is endemic within the entire US government.

One leader from Washington who did come to New York was Representative Steny Hoyer. The congressman had a reputation for supporting the Secret Service, and he made multiple visits to our New York office personnel, now scattered around Manhattan in various facilities, to personally express that support. This was my first contact with Representative Hoyer, whom I would later come into contact with in my political career when I endorsed his opponent in the 2012 general election for Maryland's Fifth Congressional District. Although I disagreed with Representative Hoyer politically, I never forgot his admirable dedication to our cause after those tragic events.

On a deeply personal note, I met my future wife, Paula, just days before 9/11. She worked for the Securities Industry Association (SIA), whose offices were adjacent to the World Trade Center towers. When she did not answer my calls on September 11, I feared she might have been a victim. But in a stroke of luck, she had decided at the last minute to visit her mother in Nevada and was touched by my continued messages checking on her. Her building was not damaged, but she would look down on the hallowed grounds of Ground Zero from her office from that day forward.

It was not long before New York City's nerves would be tested again and Paula's safety would motivate me to action. Only two months after the devastating September 11 terror attacks, a plane unexpectedly crashed, shortly after takeoff, into the Queens, New York, neighborhood of Rockaway.

I was in a local gym on Woodhaven Boulevard in Forest Hills, Queens, at the time of the crash and immediately felt my Secret Service pager vibrating and heard the roar of dozens of emergency vehicles screaming down the boulevard. Terrorism was immediately suspected and having no immediate reason to believe otherwise, I rushed to my car and headed to Paula's office on the edge of Ground Zero, believing it might be targeted again. I met her in her office and pleaded with her to leave with me. She reluctantly agreed and, despite her supervisor thinking I was overreacting, we hurriedly headed to my car and I drove her home. It was later discovered that a tragic combination of wind conditions and pilot error had caused the plane to crash into the Rockaway community, killing all 260 passengers and five people on the ground.

6

AN ASSASSIN AMONG US

AHIGH-LEVEL GATHERING of the United Nations General Assembly was always a logistical nightmare for the Secret Service. Planning and implementing a full-spectrum security plan for over a hundred heads of state and their spouses, along with the president of the United States, in the congested streets of New York City gives a security team limited options and is the perfect target for an assassin or terrorist. In the post-September 11 era, these complications were magnified even further. The 2002 UN General Assembly was going to be a test of the new operational techniques and contingency planning efforts the

Secret Service was implementing since the devastating 9/11 terrorist attacks.

By 2002, I had risen through the ranks quickly and was one of the senior agents in the protective intelligence squad. My new assignment after the Melville field office was the New York field office, now located in downtown Brooklyn after the destruction of our office space in 7 World Trade Center. The new field office was under construction when we moved in, and the wounds from the terrorist attacks were still very fresh with the agents in the office, making the dreary "under construction" setting more emotionally draining than any normal remodeling effort. The purple walls and abandoned equipment from the prior tenant, who had left in a hurry, gave it a distinctly unserious, noninstitutional look that only further damaged the already badly damaged sense of office morale.

When the assignments for the UN General Assembly began to filter in and Scott, the backup (a term for the second in command of each squad within a field office), posted them, we rushed to see who would be covering each dignitary. The Secret Service was an agency full of alpha males and females, and everyone in the squad was hoping to be assigned to a high-threat country. There was no greater challenge for a field office agent than to successfully conduct advance work for a foreign head of state designated as a high-threat-level protectee.

I was eager to see where I would be assigned and was elated when I saw the name of a country on the board with my name next to it whose threat level was high. This particular head of state claimed power in a coup d'état and instability was the only stable characteristic of his country at the time. My assignment was to exhaustively research the threats to this country, its leader, and the UN in general and provide a threat assessment based on all of this information so the members of the advance team could provide for appropriate countermeasures. The lead advance agent, Dave, was known for his thorough work and willingness to put in the long hours, and I was comfortable that he would use the information I provided to design an effective security plan.

I conducted approximately a week of planning for the visit and held thorough but contentious meetings with the staff of the foreign country. The staff, as did many others, wanted more cars in the motorcade than we could properly secure. Motorcade length is a symbol of power in the business and sometimes juvenile politics of dignitary protection, and the arduous negotiations to shrink the motorcade lasted for days. Despite such lengthy debates about minute details, the arrival of the protectee into the country was, thankfully, without incident.

After we were assured that the protectee was "in for the night" and would have no further movements from the hotel, I departed for my hotel room to try to get some well-earned sleep, but this was not to happen. At approximately two o'clock in the morning, my Blackberry rang and I was informed by the agent in charge of our detail, Roy, that sources were relaying newly acquired information to Secret Service headquarters about a plot to assassinate our protectee, and it was to be carried out in the next few days. Roy told me that the plan was to disguise an assassin as a member of the press traveling with the head of state and his staff and to kill him using a firearm.

Being awakened late at night with this type of information is every agent's worst nightmare. The responsibility for the life of the assigned protectee is a burden that the advance team shares collectively, but the pressure to perform is felt by each member singularly. Secret Service management does not micromanage their agents and gives them enormous responsibility, but that responsibility comes at a price. Agents have to own any failure to complete the mission at hand and failure is to be avoided at nearly any cost. I spent the next hour on the phone with Roy, talking through some enhanced security measures we would implement in an effort to foil any potential assassination plot. We had already designed and implemented a thorough press screening process to ensure they were "clean" (free of weapons or explosives), but out of an abundance of caution we decided to make some strategic alterations. I suggested to Roy that we resweep the press at every stop. Standard practice was to sweep them once and assign an agent to watch them to ensure they stayed clean. Given the grave nature of this threat and the devastating geopolitical and personal consequences if it was successful, I felt this to be a necessary inconvenience for the press and the staff, who assuredly would not be happy about the time these measures would add to the daily schedule.

The next day began with a heightened level of tension among the members of the detail. We ensured that the morning sweep of the press entourage was thorough and, to our relief, uncovered no weapons. When we arrived at the first stop and ordered the press entourage to go through another sweep, I could see the surprise in their eyes at this unusual request. Members of the press are an inherently curious group and they began to ask what was wrong. The questions multiplied at each successive stop when they were asked to repeat the security sweep process.

One of the great challenges of the Secret Service protection program is that we can never prove that we prevented an assassination. Assassins do not give you the courtesy of notifying you when you have defeated their plans. Throughout the day we noticed the press pool shrinking at each stop. We will never know for sure whether this was simply the result of a growing frustration with the suffocating security or a potential assassin being defeated by our security plan, but either way our mission was complete. We escorted the protectee back to his plane at John F. Kennedy International Airport and watched as he safely left the country, all the time keeping in mind that there are no rewards for an expected success, only punishment for failure.

7

TRAINING THE NEXT
GENERATION

I WAS ALWAYS LOOKING for activities to maintain a high degree of physical fitness and found the burgeoning mixed martial arts movement to be the perfect fit. It combined the strength and endurance of collegiate wrestling with the skill requirements of boxing and the strategic gamesmanship of Brazilian jiu-jitsu. Conveniently, in 2002, the Secret Service training center in Maryland opened up a position for a control tactics instructor. The majority of Secret Service hand-to-hand combat training focused on boxing instruction, but there were a number of tactical problems with this approach. The most basic issue was that all agents are armed with a handgun and an extendable baton to *avoid* getting into a stand-up hand-to-hand fight. Also, during training we often found that when a trainee lacked any boxing skills, usually he or she learned only one thing: how to take a good beating. Introducing mixed martial arts solved many of these problems. It was effective on the ground and it was surprisingly low impact.

Although I had only three years of experience as a special agent at the time the control tactics instructor position was announced, I decided that this would be a great opportunity to take my career on a new path. I applied for the vacant position and anxiously waited for a response. Marty, my former supervisor from the Melville field office, was helpful and made a number of phone calls to headquarters personnel on my behalf. Such calls are a sad but necessary part of the Secret Service culture. Merit comprises about 70 percent of the selection process for any position within the Secret Service, but the other 30 percent is having the right person make the right phone call at the right time. This is by no means a job characteristic unique to the Secret Service; within government employment there is a heavy premium placed on making the appropriate connections in order to advance your career. Thick bureaucracies within the federal government are infamous for this type of organizational advancement. Here's the way it works: government employee A promotes his friend, the less senior government employee B, into a position knowing that when government employee A retires and moves into either a lobbying or private sector position where he can leverage his inside connections, he can then rely on government employee B to provide him access to government contacts and largesse.

The personal side to my potential transfer was going to be more challenging. Paula and I were still dating at that time, and despite some initial setbacks, our relationship was getting stronger. Paula was very happy living in New York and feared the ramifications for our relationship if I moved away without her. She always told me, *"amor de lejos es amor de pendejos,"* which is an old, slightly off-color Spanish expression meaning "love from afar is love for fools." This neatly summed up her attitude about long-distance relationships.

I decided to wait until I was notified of a decision before I said anything to her about the job. In the late fall of 2002, I received a call from

Marty congratulating me on my transfer to the James J. Rowley Secret Service Training Center, located in Prince George's County, Maryland. I was ecstatic but at the same time anxious about how Paula would respond, because I would not leave without her. I immediately called her and after some tiptoeing around the issue I said, "I've been sent to DC."

Gauging by the delay in her response, I assumed she was upset. I was surprised and thrilled to hear some excitement in her voice and that she was ready for a bold change as well. Though we were dating for only a year, she said she would ask her supervisor at the SIA to see if a transfer to their Washington, DC, office would be possible. She also agreed to accompany me on my house-hunting trip to Maryland. I knew if she left me that the devastation would be permanent and was relieved at her willingness to "take a look" at Maryland.

After doing an exhaustive cost-benefit analysis of living in Maryland versus living in Virginia or Washington, I decided on Maryland. The state seemed ideal to me. Robert Ehrlich had just been elected its first Republican governor in over thirty years and, although the legislature was largely dominated by Democrats, the state itself offered a little bit of everything: good schools, a major city in Baltimore, proximity to my workplace, Catoctin Mountain Park, Deep Creek Lake, the Chesapeake Bay, Annapolis, and a whole lot more I would come to discover while living there.

Paula and I left for our house-hunting trip in November of 2002 excited at the possibilities. Owning a home was something I had never considered during my childhood and now I was taking a trip to buy one; it was a new adventure for both of us. After a long week of looking at various houses in a number of different neighborhoods, we settled on a home in Severna Park. With its white exterior, blue shutters, and spacious front lawn, it was the piece of middle-class heaven both Paula and I had been searching for our entire lives.

I moved to Maryland, initially, by myself while Paula stayed back in New York for an additional month finishing her work for the New York office of SIA. I reported to work anxious to get started in the control tactics section, but was dismayed to be temporarily assigned to the investigative tactics section. The section was short personnel and I was to fill in as an instructor until they could find a permanent replacement.

Having just completed a nearly two-year investigation of a major credit card fraud ring with a tie to international terrorism, I was well versed in the nuances of major federal investigations. After teaching classes for a week, with no prior experience at lecturing, the supervisor of the section, Bob, was impressed with my grasp of the subject matter and I was transferred to the section full time. I took on the new assignment with vigor. I enjoyed working for Bob—he had been working for the Secret Service for nearly two decades within our investigative branches and on the Vice Presidential Protective Division (VPD). Bob was always smiling, a contrast from Marty who seemed to always be internally deliberating about something. Bob had come from the VPD and in the culture of the Secret Service you are either a Presidential Protective Division (PPD) agent or you were VPD, and this label was permanent. It did not matter if you worked VPD as a rank-and-file agent and then received a promotion and moved to the PPD as a supervisor—you would always be remembered as a "VP guy."

The training center's investigative tactics training program needed a complete overhaul. With the assignment of another new agent to the section, a tough-as-nails Marine veteran named Tim, we were ready to discard the old program and start fresh. Tim and I had very different backgrounds but became quick friends. He was a country kid and I was a New Yorker, so he referred to me as "Big City." I laughed at the name and learned to live with it. Having grown up largely within the borders of New York City, I was amused by Tim's stories of shooting squirrels in his backyard with a .22 rifle as a young child. This type of activity would have led to your arrest in New York City and was unheard of. Ironically, although we grew up in polar opposite environments, we both had relatively similar worldviews and similar instruction styles. We both valued leadership and personal responsibility among the students and would reward those who may not have been the most skilled but displayed the greatest character.

Tim and I agreed that if we were going to rewrite this training program, we were going to make it state of the art. We sought out the best personnel for each specific subject area and attended training programs to learn the most updated investigative tactics in the field. Tim attended an interview and interrogation school in Florida, while I attended a surveillance school run by a prominent intelligence agency. We both solicited help from the Drug Enforcement Administration in rewriting the program's undercover tactics section. The redesign was a yearlong project and we both felt much pride in the end result, which took the best pieces of information from talented subject matter experts and created a high-quality training program.

Redesigning the curriculum was not our only responsibility, as it was expected that after an initiation period each instructor would become a class coordinator and manage a recruit class. The responsibility of managing your own class of recruits was a cherished one in the training center. Most federal agencies relegated this responsibility exclusively to supervisory staff, but the Secret Service allowed nonsupervisory personnel to perform the task with the idea that it taught and reinforced leadership skills for the students as well as the trainers.

The pressure on instructors was great and there were no excuses if your class failed to perform to the required standards. Trainees would not hesitate to destroy your credibility in their evaluations if you were not attentive and effective, and this was a significant factor in motivating the instructor staff to provide an ongoing, quality product. This experience was to teach me more about leadership than my entire body of experience to that point. I quickly learned that ranks and titles do not make men or women effective leaders. My first few months with the class, many of whom who were significantly older than I was, were tumultuous. I moved between a desire to be everyone's friend, to anger and frustration when some would take advantage of my friendly demeanor. Learning the delicate balance between goodwill and perceived weakness is a lesson that cannot be learned in a textbook.

Leadership in the real world is not pretty or glamorous, but it is deeply rewarding. I learned toward the conclusion of the trainee's program that leadership is not easily compartmentalized into flashy sound bites or a slogan on a poster. It requires the ability to allow people to cry when they need it, and to tell them to stop crying when they don't. Being an effective leader means having the ability to tell those you like that they are wrong and those you don't that they are right, and to show your human failings when there is a lesson to be transmitted. The class graduated from the Secret Service training center with their heads held high, and I graduated from the management school of life with a fresh new outlook on how to lead and, more importantly, how not to.

8

DIGNITARY PROTECTION AND THE FIGHT TO PROTECT

AFTER THREE YEARS instructing and managing new recruits at the training center, it was comforting to know that my turn to join the elite Presidential Protective Division was approaching. It is a little-known fact that very few members of the Secret Service reach the ranks of the president's protection detail. It is the ultimate career achievement for a Secret Service agent to protect the president and is held in even higher esteem than a promotion. I worked hard to reach the point where I was in a position to be considered and had one more step in front of me before I could join the elite PPD. Each agent was assigned to the Dignitary Protective Division (DPD) first for a "trial run" before being selected for either the president's or vice president's protection details.

This was a new requirement and though it was the last step until I could reach my ultimate goal, it was going to add months and potentially years of additional protection time to my career, a prospect I was not looking forward to. An agent's time on a protection detail, regardless of who the protectee is, is the most stressful portion of his service. It involves travel to extremely dangerous parts of the world with limited protection for yourself, extremely early wake-up times, long periods without eating or drinking or access to bathrooms, and a life that revolves around the schedule of the protectee and not your own. In addition, the sacrifices your family is either willingly or unwillingly co-opted into are enormous. No family event is sacred within the Secret Service, and "luxuries" like attending your children's birthday parties or watching the joy in their eyes as they open gifts on Christmas mornings always take a backseat to your duties.

There are various positions within the DPD and I was hastily assigned to the operations section. I was selected for this position because of my experience in the operations section of the training center, and it was common knowledge in the Secret Service that once you were labeled as a quality "ops guy," it stuck with you. This was going to be different for me, though. The operations section in the training center required me to handle scheduling issues and trainee affairs, not protection logistics. I had never been assigned to a full-time protective detail before and had little knowledge or on-the-job training with regard to managing its operations. I began to feverishly research the job requirements and make calls to friends for advice. Protection details are unique operational outfits that have their own jargon, rules (both stated and tacit), and codes of conduct, and agents can quickly determine who is fit to be there and who is not. I was absolutely determined to fit in and was not going to be a cautionary tale told to other agents transferred to the section.

In the winter of 2005 I reported to the DPD operations section in the middle of a midterm election and some staff shake-ups in the Bush administration. These staff changes usually had a profound impact on the agents of the DPD. The agent's lives centered around learning to predict and adapt to the behavior of a protectee, a skill that can take years, and their replacement started the entire cycle over. Every time my phone rang in the DPD, it was an issue that the caller wanted handled "immediately" and I learned to produce results quickly. I found myself glued to a phone and a desk for hours at a time, calling our various field offices all over the country and giving them the bad news that one of our protectees was headed for their districts.

Many of the field offices I dealt with on a daily basis were located in very busy areas of the country for both protection and criminal investigations, and every visit by a protectee under the management of the DPD was an additional task for them. Arrogance was a common complaint leveled against operations agents in the Secret Service, mostly due to the fact that we were handing out the orders even though we had no formal supervisory status. Having never worked on a protective detail and being responsible for guiding some of our experienced supervisors in the field through the process of protection operations was uncomfortable at times. I felt that I lacked credibility with them, but I did my best to help without coming across as arrogant, a skill some others could not pull off.

We always had the cable news channels on the office television in the DPD operations section to ensure we never missed a breaking news event. I would listen to the news playing all day and my interest in political races grew as a result. One race I found particularly interesting was the US Senate race in Maryland between former lieutenant governor Michael Steele and Representative Ben Cardin (my future political opponent). It was a political battle in a blue state in an election year that was shaping up to be a historic one for the Democratic Party. I was impressed by Steele's ability to remain competitive given all the factors working against him and I followed the race closely, hoping for a victory for Maryland Republicans that would never come.

The monotony of spending hours on the phone and computer accompanied by the lack of time in the field performing protection-related functions was beginning to drain my motivation. I had always prided myself on operational effectiveness, and manning a desk was atrophying not only my skills but my mind. I asked DPD management if I could be assigned temporarily to a protective detail to sharpen my security skills and they obliged by assigning me to secure two foreign hotels for Department of Homeland Security secretary Michael Chertoff. The first was the

Imperial Hotel in Tokyo, Japan, and the second was the Shangri-La in Beijing, China.

Securing hotels according to Secret Service standards is one of the most difficult tasks we perform and I was excited, yet anxious, about the opportunity. Doing two consecutive security advances on the opposite side of the globe as a reintroduction to operational advance work was a formidable task. I did as much research on the two hotels as I could from my desk in the DPD office and prepared for the long trip.

Upon arriving in Japan and beginning the assignment, I discovered why hotels had historically presented us with such difficulty. (Consider, for example, the Ronald Reagan shooting at the Washington, DC, Hilton, and the attempt on President Gerald Ford outside of the St. Francis Hotel in San Francisco.) Hotels are cavernous structures designed to keep employees and equipment hidden from sight. The cleaning and maintenance staff navigate a circuitous route of hidden hallways allowing them to move freely around the hotel out of sight of the guests. This is an assassin's dream and a Secret Service agent's worst nightmare. We have the advantage in any location where we have familiarity with the terrain, such as the White House, but in a hotel agents have a limited period of time to become as familiar with the landscape as they are with the White House.

The advance at the Imperial Hotel was exhausting as I acclimated to the time change and walked miles each day through its corridors and up and down its stairwells. Secretary Chertoff's visit was thankfully uneventful, and with no break I boarded a plane and traveled to China. The dynamic between the Secret Service and the staff at the Shangri-La in Beijing was very different from the dynamic we shared with the Imperial in Tokyo. The Imperial staff allowed us open and unimpeded access to all areas within the hotel, and they found us amusing with the detailed questions we would pose to them. We would walk through the kitchens and the rear hallways and became a fixture within the hotel during our time there.

I found the security staff at the Shangri-La more restrictive and cautious with our access, which was in line with the country's generally skeptical view of foreign security. They allowed me to walk through the hotel, but I was confronted at every corner by a different security staff representative and had to constantly repeat my intentions at each turn. It was frustrating and impressive at the same time. The intense security added hours to what

should have been a relatively routine advance at the Shangri-La, but it would
work to my benefit during the visit and I was confident in their ability to
control access to the hotel areas we were most concerned about. I logically
assumed that if I couldn't navigate a corridor without being confronted at
every terrain feature, then neither could a hypothetical assassin.

The trip was successful, but more importantly for me it was a crash
course in protection that I needed to prepare for my next assignment, the
Presidential Protective Division.

In the late spring of 2006 I heard through office gossip that another
round of transfers to the PPD was about to commence. Any talk about
transfers to the PPD was always the source of temporary chaos. If any agents
suspected or heard that they were being transferred to the vice president's
detail and had worked diligently to get to the PPD, the phone calls would
start. They would call any management-level official they knew to ensure
that this did not happen. I had not heard from anyone regarding my status
and started to consider how to tell Paula if I was not selected for the PPD.
Being with me every step of the way, she would be as devastated as I was if
I wasn't selected for the PPD, as she knew how important it was to me. We
had been together since the attacks of 9/11 and she was more supportive of
my career aspirations than I could have ever dreamed. My fears were allayed
late one evening in May of 2006 while I was standing on the front lawn of
Department of Homeland Security secretary Michael Chertoff's home in the
dark. My flashlight battery was running low as I made my routine security
check around the house, so I used my Secret Service–issued Blackberry
for illumination. As I looked at the screen I saw a new message. It was my
official transfer to the Presidential Protective Division.

9

THE "BIG SHOW": THE PRESIDENTIAL PROTECTIVE DIVISION

EVERY SECRET SERVICE AGENT'S FIRST DAY at the White House as part of the PPD is a surreal experience. Walking through the claustrophobia-inducing hallways of the West Wing and bumping shoulders with the nation's most powerful men and women is an experience most can only imagine from what they've seen on television. Yet I was immediately plunged into the operational security workings of the president's detail with little time for reflection on my surroundings.

My first shift at the White House began in the early afternoon. I walked into our West Wing office and immediately ran into a friend of mine from the New York office, who had just completed his first shift, and was shocked to find out that he was assigned to a post directly with the president. I clearly remember him saying to me with a slightly over-whelmed look, "Wow, it's real now."

I spent the majority of my first day in the White House mentally rehearsing the security plan that was still relatively new to me and trying to take in the fear and elation of being part of "the big show." The White House is a complicated structure, with a very detailed and layered security plan, and ensuring that my reaction to an incident would become second nature was a responsibility I took very seriously. The responses to any series of incidents at the White House are not simple "if A happens, then do B" action steps. They require careful analysis and deliberative thought, features not inherent in any high-stress attack scenario.

In order to avoid any hesitation of action, the Secret Service agents of the PPD are constantly rehearsing the multilayered responses to any potential scenario requiring action. Because of this, the Secret Service was hesitant to send agents new to the PPD outside the White House grounds until they had accumulated some experience with the internal dynamics of the detail; therefore I knew I would have the opportunity to process the security protocol inside the White House before being asked to take on more responsibility. Presidential security is such a complicated endeavor, involving so many different variables, that I had to be cautious not to get too far ahead of myself but to focus on performing the task at hand each day to the best of my ability.

In addition to the endless security plans to memorize, agents new to the PPD also had to learn a series of unwritten rules. Mastering the unwritten rules was as complicated as mastering the written ones, and the penalties for violating them were severe. One of those inviolable rules was to never be caught on the White House grounds dressed in anything but business attire unless it was the dress code for the day (e.g., golf with the president). Punishment for breaking this rule was a string of bad assign-ments, so it was a mistake usually made only once. Another unwritten rule was to never engage the protectee in an unsolicited conversation. Any agent who could not fight an urge to start a conversation with the president would see his time on the detail cut short.

Arguably, the most important rule was to never, ever, be caught complaining about the detail. Developing a reputation as a whiner was a death sentence for an agent's career. Word spread quickly on the PPD and once it was out there, a bad reputation was hard to shake. The peer pressure enforcing these rules, both written and unwritten, was intense, and I learned to adjust my behavior accordingly.

After a two-month period working on President George W. Bush's shift and experiencing the intense heat at his Waco ranch, the difficulties of changing from a suit to ranch attire in the bathroom of Air Force One, learning how to open the doors of the presidential limo (it is not easy), constantly battling for parking on the White House grounds, and the zero tolerance for whining and complaining, the indoctrination process was complete and I was promptly transferred to the security detail of Jenna Bush.

All new PPD agents had to complete an assignment on one of the Bush daughter details, after a two-month assignment to the presidential shift, as part of the PPD career track. These smaller details are less regimented, and developing personal relationships with the protectees, although frowned upon, is not uncommon. I found Jenna to be affable, kind, and extremely adventurous, and I heard from agents on the detail that she had an intense travel schedule planned over the course of the next year—a fact my wife found disturbing, as Paula had become accustomed to my consistent work hours and a lighter travel load through my time in the DPD and at the training center. The schedule centered around a book Jenna was writing regarding her experiences with an HIV-positive woman named Ana while working with UNICEF. We were scheduled to travel to South America for an extended stay right after a road trip across the United States she was planning shortly after my arrival.

Working as an agent on Jenna's detail was interesting because the security footprint was effective but not as obvious as the president's. This lack of visible security would result in the same puzzled reaction from people who recognized her. They would see her and then proceed to scan the area for the Secret Service. When they did not immediately see us, I could read their lips as they would say, "That's not her." While following her in the vehicles on her cross-country trip it turned into a game as the agent I was assigned to partner with, Matt, and I would watch the passing vehicles do this again and again.

I enjoyed the change of pace during my first few weeks with Jenna, and not having to fight for parking on the White House ellipse and wear a business suit every day significantly reduced the stress factor. We were constantly moving, and each day was a new experience. Finding hotels to sleep in during the road trip became a daily adventure as we would drive through small towns in America most people will never visit and have likely never heard of. The two-week trip ended for us in Bandon, Oregon, a town that seemed mildly surprised at our arrival into their quiet piece of America. With a population of just over three thousand, the arrival of the frst daughter and a cadre of Secret Service agents elicited some excitement and confusion, as some were unsure if it really was Jenna Bush. When we walked into a local restaurant, it was like a scene out of a movie where the jukebox goes silent and everyone turns their attention to the front door. The locals were either delighted or astonished that we were there—either way, they treated us well and the buzz we had caused in the town was palpable as everyone we passed seemed to know who we were and gave us a not-so-subtle wink or nod. This adventurous cross-country trip was but a small taste of what was to come on our upcoming South American journey.

The first stop on Jenna's tour of South America was Panama. The agents and I planned to stay for an extended period in Panama City, and given the length of the trip we had to prepare accordingly. Items we take for granted in our daily lives become an issue when living overseas in a hotel not designed for long-term residents. Finding food, clean water, a gym, and proper medical assistance (an issue which would become critical for me shortly after arriving) were constant challenges.

Fortunately, our Panamanian security counterparts made these tasks slightly less daunting. Assigned to us twenty-four hours a day, there was very little they could not do. They seemed to be connected to a network of insiders who could acquire anything we needed. Throughout my career, I found this trait to be quite common overseas. We in the United States have a system of government where we largely do not live in fear of law enforcement. This is not the case in many other countries. I learned that a history of government oppression or internal strife left a scar of fear of law enforcement on many of the citizens of these countries. As one Panamanian told me, "Those who have the guns, have the power." This power gives law-enforcement personnel access to an influential network of people not necessarily commensurate with their position.

After a few days acclimating to the water and environment as I awaited Jenna's arrival with the team, I developed the standard gastrointestinal illness, which became a part of nearly every foreign trip I went on. But it was not long after her arrival that other problems began. The agents on Jenna's detail had, over time, become accustomed to the idiosyncrasies of working on a smaller, less regimented detail with an adventurous protectee. We knew her habits and how to communicate with her, yet PPD management decided to send an Assistant Special Agent in Charge (ASAIC) down to Panama with us to manage the operation, despite the fact that he had limited experience working with Jenna. It was not long before conflicts regarding implementation of our protection plan developed.

We had established some unique yet effective nontraditional approaches to keeping Jenna safe, and the agents on the detail and I grew frustrated with the incessant second-guessing from the ASAIC given our record of success to that point. One agent in particular, who had an outstanding reputation for honesty, was fed up and challenged the ASAIC after a week of internal bickering. The ASAIC appeared stunned when the subordinate agent confronted him forcefully. We won that exchange and the ASAIC left the country shortly thereafter, to the relief of the detail and Jenna.

The dangers of being a Secret Service agent on a foreign protection assignment are not all of the tactical variety. Before leaving for Panama, I, along with the rest of Jenna's detail, was warned about the variety of potential illnesses we could acquire in South America if we were not diligent. Malaria was still a problem and the White House Medical Unit strongly advised us to wear appropriate clothing and to liberally apply mosquito repellant. Having traveled for years with the Secret Service and never dealing with any condition worse than common gastrointestinal illnesses, I ignorantly disregarded the advice. It was a decision I would come to regret.

I was assigned to work the afternoon shift on February 4, 2007, Super Bowl Sunday, with Andrew, the agent who had greeted me at the White House during my initial shift there. Jenna was not scheduled to leave her small apartment, so we expected a slow night. We occupied the apartment directly next door and we had a small television with a picture so terrible you could barely recognize a face on the screen. Between shifts watching the apartment, we could tune in to the game and watch the Colts and

Bears fight it out for Super Bowl victory.

During the night I began to feel ill, but unlike a standard cold or flu that typically comes on slowly, I was deteriorating rapidly and within thirty minutes I felt as if I was going to lose consciousness. Mike, the acting supervisor on the trip and a very close friend from my days in the New York and Melville offices, was concerned and quickly had another agent rush to the apartment to relieve me so I could head back to the hotel. What followed was the most painful experience I ever lived through.

I had contracted dengue fever from a mosquito bite. The symptoms I experienced made it clear to me why the illness is also known as "break-bone fever." I was in and out of consciousness and alone in the hotel for the duration of the night, feeling as if my entire body was being crushed while fluctuating between extreme fever and bone-chilling shivers. I was sweating profusely and had soaked the mattress I was sleeping on, and as a result I was severely dehydrated.

When the sun rose and I began to realize the severity of my situation, I called Mike and told him what was happening. He immediately called our Miami field office, which had jurisdiction over the South American region, and asked them for help. Mike also sent Tom to pick me up and take me to a local medical facility that was woefully incompatible with American standards of medicine. Working with the Miami field office, Mike arranged for a flight and had Miami agents meet me in the airport to ensure I made it to my connecting flight home. My condition worsened on the plane and by the time I arrived home I had lost nearly fifteen pounds of fluids. Paula picked me up from the airport and cared for me. I did not return to work for three weeks, and it would be another month after that before I was back to my normal physical state.

Although the infectious disease specialist I was seeing to deal with the fallout from contracting dengue fever advised me to not return to work, after three weeks I began to grow restless. The specialist also warned me that dengue fever can be contracted again post-infection, and that the second time it could be lethal. She told me that dengue hemorrhagic fever, where severe internal bleeding results, is possible with a secondary infection and that I should avoid traveling back to South America.

Ignoring the specialist, I called PPD operations and Mike and told them to add me back into the operational shift. At this point, Jenna had left Panama and was headed to Argentina, the detail in tow, and I felt that I would be letting the team down if I chose to stay stateside on sick leave. We were a small detail, and the loss of any one agent just meant that everyone else had to pick up the slack. On PPD, we never let illness decrease our security footprint. If someone was sick, then someone else on the detail had to fill in, doubling his work hours. I decided that regardless of my weak condition I had to get back to work. I returned to a vigorous workout schedule to physically prepare myself and committed to returning to full strength before leaving for Argentina.

Argentina presented the same set of circumstances as Panama regarding food, water, and living arrangements, and it was going to be another prolonged visit. One major difference between the two countries was that Argentina would present some major security challenges compared to the relatively uneventful visit to Panama. We had been in a relatively controlled environment in Panama due to the security already in place in the area where we stayed with Jenna. (The presence of a United Nations office within our Panamanian complex came with some welcome additional security.) We had no such luxury in Argentina. The apartment Jenna chose was located off a public street and in an area of Buenos Aires that had an ongoing crime problem, and we would have to adjust accordingly.

The crime problem became evident within a few days when a Miami agent on a temporary assignment to assist us reported over the radio that a man was beating his girlfriend in front of Jenna's apartment and had pulled a knife. These occurrences were not uncommon on the block where the apartment was located, but they decreased dramatically in frequency as the locals figured out who we were and why we were there. The street-crime situation in other areas of Argentina, however, was about to become an embarrassment to the Secret Service when Jenna's sister, Barbara, decided to visit and *we* became the story.

Despite the enhanced security due to both of the president's daughters being in the country, while having coffee at an outdoor café on her first day in Buenos Aires, Barbara's purse was stolen, ostensibly off the back of her chair. I was working with Jenna, not Barbara, on the day this occurred, but I was not far from the scene and neither I nor any of the other agents recalled seeing anything unusual. Our security operation is focused strictly on proctectees, not their property, and when Barbara reported that she was missing her purse we speculated that she may have walked away from it and while our attention was on her rather than her bag, someone grabbed it.

Regardless of what really happened, the result was a media disaster that reflected poorly on the Secret Service. Management struggled with the media to explain the incident, which left me extremely frustrated. Our mission was clear, and it did not involve looking after property, only people. I had followed Jenna across the United States on the road trip, to Panama and back, and now to Argentina, and we ensured she was secure and the trips went without incident. This incident devalued that success and all of the sacrifice and hard work that went into it. I learned that when it involves public figures and politicians, quiet successes are irrelevant while perceived public failures, no matter how insignificant, are defining. The incident was further compounded when another Miami field office agent assisting us in country, despite multiple warnings not to venture out alone while off duty, did so and was assaulted, robbed, and left in the street. Combined with the stolen purse story, the media narrative was brutal. Morale within the detail was damaged, but we gave our hearts and souls to the mission and we were not going to allow it to be diminished by anyone.

The adventures with Jenna Bush continued as we traveled through South America and beyond. The first daughter was scheduled for a short trip to Kingston, Jamaica, where we were to meet with ABC's Diane Sawyer to film a profile on Jenna and discuss her upcoming book. During filming, Diane and Jenna wanted to do a shot where they were walking in an alleyway in inner Kingston. We had to secure the area while they talked and the camera crew filmed. It was not long before the area became crowded with locals, both curious and dangerous.

At that time, Kingston was the homicide capital of the world, and we were not about to contribute to that notorious statistic. Still, the security situation deteriorated quickly. Some of the locals clearly had weapons, and we were quickly being surrounded at the end of the alley with only one exit. We made the quick decision to immediately end the interview and, with weapons drawn, hurried Jenna and Diane to an armored SUV we had waiting for us.

Amazingly, the ABC camera crew appeared entirely unmoved by

what had just occurred. One of the cameramen I spoke to about the incident later that night explained to me that he was in Somalia in the days immediately prior to the *Blackhawk Down* incident and learned to just keep filming no matter what. I was impressed by his resolve. When the footage aired as part of an ABC *20/20* series months later, the tension among the agents and fear of failing in our mission to keep our protectee safe was obvious.

As my time on Jenna's detail came to a close, I was asked to think about which assignment I wanted next. As part of the PPD career track, the next phase would be one of three separate "satellites," as they were called within the detail. My choices were the first lady's protection detail, the transportation section, or the countersurveillance team. While each assignment had its advantages and disadvantages, it was widely known that the transportation section had the broadest set of responsibilities and required logistics capabilities that would be valuable in any future Secret Service assignment. I was hesitant at first to request the assignment and initially considered the first lady's detail, but after the purse snatching episode, dengue fever, and the near-death experience in Kingston, I felt it was time to move on to the next phase. I joined the transportation section, eager to start fresh.

10

TRANSPORTATION: IT'S NOT SIMPLY ABOUT MOTORCADES

THE TRANSPORTATION SECTION was a significant change in operational tempo from Jenna's detail. Our accumulating successes went largely unnoticed but our failures became perpetual fodder, largely for agents of the more glamorous first lady's detail. For this reason the transportation section tended to attract the type A personalities who preferred a high-risk/no-reward work environment. It was common knowledge that despite the incredible amount of work designing safe and efficient motorcade routes, we were rarely thanked for getting the president from point A to point B. Additionally, driving the president's limousine is one of the most stressful assignments in the detail. The media commonly referred to the limo as "the Beast," although the agents of the transportation section never use this ridiculous term and can distinguish media representatives "in the know" from those looking to appear as if they are, simply by whether or not they use that term.

While navigating an unwieldy armored limousine, the agent driving must be ready at any moment to take one of the alternate motorcade routes and know all the relocation points and safe zones, all while attempting to avoid rear-ending the car in front of him and subsequently having to answer questions from the detail supervisor and the president. Although frequently an error-free exercise, hiccups are not uncommon, and with the White House press corps always in tow, they are always on tape for the world to see. Some of the more famous footage, immortalized on YouTube, includes one of our presidential limos stalling on a street in Italy filled with enormous crowds, and one of the limos striking a security gate that failed to lower in Ireland and subsequently stranding the entire motorcade behind it.

Despite thousands of uneventful motorcades due to the preparation and dedication of the men and women of the transportation section, these very public failures have become cautionary tales for new agents. Secret Service headquarters fears public embarrassment even if the actual security ramifications are minimal, and with a minimal public relations machine (unlike the FBI, who have greater manpower and therefore greater ability to handle public relations), they frequently make an example of agents whom they deem responsible for high-profile failures. This would come to haunt any agent associated with the devastating Colombian prostitution scandal of 2012.

With the consequences of failure always weighing heavily on my mind, I dedicated myself entirely to learning the detailed nuances of conducting transportation advances for the president. As with everything else on the PPD, the transportation section brought their agents along slowly and gave the newer agents the easier assignments first. They also ensured that a more experienced agent from the section guided the newer agents through the elaborate planning process.

My first advance was what we called an "in-town." This was the term used to describe a motorcade strictly within the borders of Washington, DC, and although the planning was intense, the trips were easier logistically and were typically the first assignments for newer agents. In-towns were typically conducted with both Secret Service personnel and law-enforcement agencies who were intimately familiar with the operational requirements of the PPD and could handle the task without much coaching. Although my first trip was an in-town, it was a long trip to Walter Reed Hospital. The route to the hospital was just within the parameters for driving rather than taking the presidential helicopter, Marine One, and was going to require enormous numbers of police personnel to ensure a safe and secure route.

In preparation, I drove the planned motorcade route tirelessly, familiarizing myself with every nook and crevice on the road and in the surrounding areas. After spending days in the planning phase preparing for contingencies, I was anxious for "game day," a term Secret Service agents use to describe the day of the presidential visit. I immediately sensed a problem when I walked out of the White House's Diplomatic Reception Room and didn't recognize the police officer assigned to drive the lead police vehicle. My concerns were confirmed when only a few minutes into the twenty-minute trip, he picked up a paper copy of the route from the console, jammed it against the steering wheel, and begin to feverishly flip through the pages. I immediately recognized that he did not know the route and I told him to put the paperwork down and that I would guide him. The feeling of profound relief when we arrived at Walter Reed was unforgettable, and I was quietly thankful that I had driven the route often enough to navigate it practically blindfolded. During the advance I was assisted by Tim, my coworker and friend from the training center, who had arrived in the transportation section a few weeks before I did and was still calling me "Big City." Tim was a fast learner and had cautioned me not to rely on anyone else to know the motorcade route, which obviously paid dividends on this particular trip.

After successfully planning and implementing the Walter Reed Hospital in-town visit, I was given my first out-of-town assignment to Lancaster, Pennsylvania. The logistics of the trip would be made easier given the short distance from the Washington metropolitan area. Visits in proximity to the Washington, DC, area, such as this one, enabled us to drive to the locations using Secret Service vehicles and eliminated the hassle of flying and renting vehicles.

We left Washington and arrived in Lancaster just a few hours later, checked into the hotel, and prepared to work. The first step in any visit outside of Washington is the police meeting, a gathering of all the police agencies and emergency personnel in the area, where all the agents (including the transportation agent) provide detailed briefings on what exactly we do and what we need from them. This was the first police meeting where I was going to be presenting material and, while sitting in the room waiting for the meeting to begin, I recalled my first police meeting while assigned to the Melville office. Scott from the Hillary Clinton detail had presented a polished and professional brief that garnered him instant respect from the police officials, and the memory of it weighed heavily on me. I rehearsed my presentation quietly to ensure smooth recollection of the material, and when it was my turn I took the floor confidently.

After the meeting concluded, I met privately with select supervisory police personnel and the Secret Service lead advance and asked that they consider relaying to PPD operations that we use Marine One to fly rather than drive to the first Lancaster site on the schedule. I felt that a Marine One helicopter lift would ensure a minimal disruption of traffic patterns and allow President Bush to land right across the street from the plant we were visiting. My concerns were taken into account but I was told that due to logistics concerns we were going to have to use the armored vehicles to drive from the airport to the Lancaster site.

On the day of the visit, as we transported the president from the landing zone to the plant, I noticed traffic begin to back up quickly on the other side of the road. As the motorcade continued on, the traffic situation worsened significantly. We were all acutely aware that President Bush could see what we all could see, a traffic tie-up for miles, and the president always insisted on minimal disruptions to the citizens of the areas he chose to visit.

I was comfortable enough with the layered security plan to make some changes to allow some of the traffic to filter off the highway and, by the time we arrived at the plant, I was changing our route for the return trip to ensure we avoided the traffic problem on the way back. I had planned for a number of alternate routes and although moving the police personnel and security measures along the route was difficult, within a few minutes I had the process on the path to completion. The Pennsylvania State Police were frustrated at the changes but security is a complicated game, and after profuse apologies we had an uneventful and traffic-free return trip, sparing the president any bad press and me the voluminous paperwork explaining away why we shut down nearly a quarter of the town's roads during rush hour.

The transportation section had a wide range of responsibilities in addition to its primary role of providing for secure motorcade routes. Some of my fondest memories on the PPD occurred while assigned to the transportation section but while involved in some of our additional responsibilities.

Unlike some of the other satellite details within the PPD, the agents of the transportation section are consistently working within the bubble surrounding the president. We had regular assignments at the White House, and we traveled on foreign presidential trips to provide logistics support, giving us an inside view to the presidency the public never sees, and some of which it does.

A few months in, I was given an assignment at the White House and was privileged to witness an event few see from the inside but many see from the outside. An Oval Office speech is an event typically reserved for only the most solemn of presidential addresses. It is a tool used sparingly and when it is used the magnificence of the office is meant to magnify and echo the message. Nearly everyone of my generation remembers Ronald Reagan's Oval Office address after the space shuttle *Challenger* disaster. His moving speech served to comfort a grieving nation.

In September of 2007, I stood outside the thick white door to the Oval Office and watched as President George W. Bush spoke to the world from the iconic Oval Office desk, constructed of wood from the British exploration ship *Resolute*, about the War on Terror in Iraq. After working in the White House and for the Secret Service for close to a decade at this point, there were few events that really got my attention emotionally. But standing there, a city kid who grew up above a bar eating Cheerios for dinner, now looking directly at the president of the United States as he addressed hundreds of millions of people about a seminal event in our time, was an especially poignant moment in my life.

The stress of working in the transportation section is magnified during the end of a president's second term. Presidents often conduct international "farewell tours" as their time in office comes to an end, and foreign trips are very labor-intensive from a security perspective. Collaboration and planning with foreign security, police, and military personnel is very different from planning a visit with state police or local emergency personnel in the United States. In some foreign countries, the standards and training levels for their personnel and readiness of their equipment are very different from the standards in the US. When conducting a security advance for the president in a foreign country, questions such as "Is this bridge structurally stable?" are not uncommon. It would be senseless to secure a motorcade route if the roads and infrastructure cannot handle the weight of the presidential limo and could potentially collapse when we drive over them. Driving in foreign countries can also be perilous due to the often chaotic, disorganized traffic patterns, something we are not accustomed to in the US.

Although we clear the roadways for the president, a number of events have happened behind the scenes that are less glamorous and create uniquely stressful situations. I vividly recall a January 2008 trip President George W. Bush took to the Middle East where I was relocated at the last minute to provide support in Dubai and Abu Dhabi, United Arab Emirates. I had been in Kuwait transporting President Bush, Secretary of State Condoleezza Rice, and General David Petraeus from Kuwait City to Camp Arifjan and immediately upon returning was told by our DC team to quickly fly to Abu Dhabi to provide assistance. They were short manpower and needed to immediately get the armored vehicles relocated to Dubai. Upon landing we sprinted to the vehicles and at maximum speed with a police escort, we drove the highways of the UAE, setting off nearly every speed camera from Abu Dhabi to Dubai. It looked like a red carpet with paparazzi camera flashes, but if those vehicles had failed to arrive in time the mission would have collapsed.

The many complications of foreign advance work were on my mind as I was sent overseas to conduct my first foreign transportation advance for First Lady Laura Bush in Petra, Jordan. My initial impression of the Jordanian security services was that they were experienced at threat assessment and were eager to help provide for a secure visit for the first lady. Their briefings were thorough and professional, and the trip was going to require the standard twelve- to sixteen-hour workdays, which were typical for a foreign advance, but I was eager to start and just as eager to see an area of the world considered an international treasure, the Lost City of Petra.

The Lost City of Petra was carved into the stone on the sides of deep cliffs in the Jordanian desert, and the detail in the enormous structures is mesmerizing. This remarkable achievement in preindustrial engineering was also made famous as the fictional Canyon of the Crescent Moon in the movie *Indiana Jones and the Last Crusade*.

Clearance to negotiate our armored vehicles through the Siq, a long pathway cut deep through the cavern, was a point of serious contention for the Jordanians, who preferred that no vehicles be allowed on this hallowed ground. But with the elevated threat level on the visit, I could not allow the first lady to walk such a distance without access to an armored means of evacuation. The threat of a coordinated assault on the motorcade on the razor-thin roads of Petra by regional extremists was very real on this trip.

The Jordanians agreed to provide heavy weapons, loaded on the backs of armored SUVs, as a readily visible deterrent, but these were deemed unacceptable by the White House staff back in the US. Photographs of belt-fed weapons on the first lady's motorcade don't make for positive political images in the American media. Given the extraordinary threat levels, I insisted on having enough firepower to counter any potential small arms attack, and after some labored negotiating with the staff, they complied.

It was an unforgettable sight on the day of the visit as Mrs. Bush arrived from Amman via helicopter and we drove her to Petra. Emerging from the long Siq and having the bright desert sun shining down on Al Khazneh (the Treasury) with the long motorcade of sophisticated, armored protection vehicles and hordes of Jordanian and American security representatives was an incredible visual contrast of the old and new world. The negotiating skills I employed on this trip would serve me well on my next foreign transportation advance in an area of the world presenting me with a completely different set of concerns: Paris, France.

President Bush's trip to Paris in the closing months of his presidency was fraught with difficulty from the start. Most of the motorcade routes that my French security counterparts proposed involved either crossing over or driving down the Champs Élysées, one of the most famous streets in the world and a major, crowded tourist attraction in Paris. In my analysis of the security situation, I felt strongly that we could not provide adequate security without closing the street to vehicle traffic. The French strongly objected to my approach and were adamant that it could not be done. Compounding the difficulty was the notification I had received that the president wanted to take a bike ride somewhere in Paris. Planning for these bike rides was challenging in the United States but was nearly impossible overseas. President Bush was a skilled cross-country bicyclist, and securing a large enough area for him to ride within the confines of the city of Paris was a challenge. While in Washington, DC, the president typically rode his bike at military facilities that obviously had a high degree of security, a luxury we would not have in Paris.

After a week of negotiations between me, the Secret Service lead advance agent, John, and the French, they acquiesced to our request to close the Champs Élysées, which solved one problem. But the security of the bike ride was still an unresolved issue.

I asked an agent on the advance team named Frank to pick a location for the bike ride and to develop a plan to secure it. He assured me that the route he ultimately selected was secure and we felt comfortable with our plan. During the outing, our confidence quickly turned to panic as the president rode off the specified bike route at his typical fast pace and we had a difficult time keeping visual contact with him from the road. My heart rate accelerated rapidly as I thought to myself, *Please do not lose the president.*

My fear grew with each second I was "in the blind." Then I heard the voice of the Secret Service supervisor working the bike ride in my earpiece saying something every agent dreads: "Where is the president?"

Angry and frustrated that they had deviated from the route we had planned, I prepared for a response and was readying to take responsibility for the mishap when the president and the agents riding with him emerged from the wooded area to the left of our vehicles. I calmly responded, "At our twelve o'clock, sir."

Relieved, but still infuriated that we deviated from our plan, I thanked my French security counterparts who managed to keep pace with the president and privately concluded that I would never place that degree of trust in another agent again. "Trust, but personal follow-up" became my credo, and it would serve me well throughout my career.

11

THE PRESIDENT'S
LIFE IN MY HANDS

AFTER YEARS WORKING DILIGENTLY through the ranks of the
Secret Service in order to be selected for the Presidential Protective Division, I found that there is no competitive respite
when you arrive there. A very small group of agents is selected for the PPD,
and even fewer are selected as lead advance agents for the president, the
highest level of operational achievement. One misstep and your chances
at being selected as a lead advance agent are finished. Unlike many top-
heavy departments within our federal government, the Secret Service
has a flat management structure, and it pushes an enormous amount of

responsibility down to its detail agents. Lead advance agents are given the sole responsibility for the overall security plan and are ultimately responsible for ensuring the safety of the president on any visit outside the White House grounds. Managing an entire advance team, monitoring the security budget, and serving as the face of the White House in conjunction with the White House staff is an honor and a privilege, and I was determined to exceed expectations.

I was selected for the lead advance training course after successfully completing a second assignment in the transportation section as the "Whip" (a quasi-supervisory position). The selection list is published on the agency's e-mail system and is a public acknowledgment of a successful body of work. Attending the lead advance training course is no guarantee of being selected, however, and many agents "die on the vine," meaning they are trained but never given the chance to actually conduct a lead advance. I was selected for a number of interim assignments after successfully completing the training course, and they all were challenging, but my first assignment enabled me to witness a transformative event in our collective US history firsthand: I was asked to handle the security for the PPD for newly elected president Barack Obama's walk down the Inaugural parade route.

My involvement in this event transformed the way in which I viewed security for crowded outdoor events. It was a learning experience I was to speak of frequently in media appearances years later, after the tragic bombings at the Boston Marathon in 2013. President Obama's election as the forty-fourth president of the United States marked a historic moment and I was proud to be a part of it, despite our legions of political differences.

President-elect Obama's inauguration was going to require an elaborate security plan and I was honored to play a pivotal role in its implementation. The Secret Service and the Presidential Inaugural Committee (PIC) knew this event was historic and that the crowd size would be unprecedented. The law-enforcement and military assets dedicated to securing this event were incomparable. Law-enforcement officers were transported in from all over the United States, and military personnel from specialized teams were deployed to strategic locations in Washington, DC.

Although the security operation we planned was impressive, I could see the apprehension in the eyes of the PPD management team when I briefed them in a secure room hidden in a dark corner of the eighteen acres of the White House complex. It was not a look I was used to. Everyone in the room knew that the president was going to exit the safe confines of our tank-like armored presidential limousine and walk the parade route, despite any misgivings we may have had about it, and the concerns were very real. Securing an entire street in Washington, DC, and guaranteeing the same level of security provided on the White House grounds is an enormous security undertaking, and if just one weapon managed to slip into our secure zone, a historic tragedy was virtually guaranteed.

The questions from the management team came quickly and covered such areas as tactical countermeasures to an armed assault, medical response, chemical and biological mitigation measures, explosive detection, airborne attack, and many others. I prepared extensively for the briefing, almost as if I were preparing for a difficult college final exam, and answered each question in detail to assuage their fears. I was comfortable with the planning and had walked through the site and the location of all our emergency and law-enforcement assets many times, always keeping in mind the grave consequences of any security failure.

The size of the crowd on Inauguration Day 2009 did not disappoint. In my ten years with the Secret Service to that point, I had attended many high-profile events, yet nothing compared to this. I arrived at 3:00 a.m. and immediately began checking that every door was locked, every window was closed, every magnetometer was working, and every agent was prepared.

It was an unusually cold day and the suit I was wearing did little to block the penetrating wind. As the hours passed, I could barely feel my extremities as the cold pavement of Pennsylvania Avenue drove straight through the leather soles of my shoes. The sun rising in the morning provided a small degree of relief, but that relief was short-lived as we were met by a rush of people waiting to be screened by our magnetometers— screening I would experience for myself as a civilian media commentator for President Obama's 2012 inauguration.

The security lines to access Pennsylvania Avenue grew by the minute and were becoming increasingly difficult to control. The calls for assistance from agents assigned to my zone were endless, and I believe we were saved only by the gracious nature of the impressive crowd. The crowds remained calm and in good spirits, despite the long lines, and the atmosphere inside the secure zone was festive.

Although I had staunchly supported Senator John McCain during the election, I felt pride in my country that day. A presidential inauguration is not the time to fight a political fight. I heard the newly inaugurated president's speech booming over the speakers placed around the city and watched as many of the people in the crowd began to cry. Some of those people did not need to read about the civil rights era in textbooks; they had lived through the pain and indignity of that era, and although those are wounds that may heal, the scars will never disappear. Witnessing the joy in their eyes as they stood in the bitter cold, listening to the words of our first African American president, is an image I will never forget.

It also changed me politically. I came to the painful realization that my political party had done a poor job both acknowledging the lasting scars left behind by this dark period in our collective American history, and communicating the message about their integral role in ending it. Thankfully, most of us will never experience the indignity of institutional racism, but we must, as a country, never forget that the power of government has not always been a repository of good intentions.

It was not long after the conclusion of President Obama's speech that he moved down the parade route toward my security zone. Working since three in the morning, I was confident that we were ready and I rehearsed the emergency response in my head over and over as he approached. In my earpiece I heard Don, the detail leader, say, "Bongino, coming to you."

The crowd erupted as the president exited the vehicle with First Lady Michelle Obama and began his walk. The sea of camera flashes was nearly blinding and the excited crowd made it difficult to hear Don through my earpiece. I reassured him that everything was secure as he kept his eyes virtually glued to the president. This was Don's last time working as a detail leader for the PPD and he was not going to allow any security lapses. Each step of the president's walk seemed to last an eternity and I was anxious to see him leave my zone of responsibility and enter the viewing stand located just outside the north grounds of the White House. As I watched him leave my area of responsibility safely, I felt a deep sense of satisfaction with the success of the mission and the Secret Service's role in it.

The media would report later on significant inauguration crowd-control issues in the Washington, DC, Third Street Tunnel, an incident that later became known as the "Purple Tunnel of Doom," where numerous "Purple Ticket" holders were denied access. It turned out that the Capitol Police and the Secret Service had two completely different ideas of the role of the tunnel in the overall protection plan, despite months of planning and coordination. This incident was an embarrassment for the Secret Service but the lapse was not with security; it was a logistics and crowd-control failure. This is not meant to minimize the significance of its impact but to discriminate between operational security failures and organizational failures. Having lived through the experience, I attribute the tunnel failure to a recurrent theme within this book: an overly bureaucratic and unnecessarily segmented federal law-enforcement workforce that has a difficult time with interagency communications and coordination, despite the best of intentions.

These problems are all too common and are entirely preventable, but not as our federal government is currently organized. Every additional agency we create in turn creates another agency head whose interests are in protecting its department, its people, and its budget. As a result, missions consistently suffer because the incentives are wrong. Managers think they are doing their duty to protect "their agency" and "their people" when they are really employees of the American people and there to serve a larger mission. These incentives will never change until we pursue a complete overhaul of our federal law-enforcement architecture with a consolidation of agencies and bureaucratic layers. This can be accomplished only through a broad-based initiative designed to allocate scarce taxpayer dollars to law-enforcement priorities rather than individual agency priorities.

The assignment that followed President Obama's first inauguration was not nearly as historic, but the safety of the president is not tied to any history lesson. The president had scheduled a number of trips outside the White House grounds postinauguration as part of his effort to grow in the role, and I was to be a part of one of them.

When I received a phone call from the operations section regarding a presidential visit to Trinidad, I knew it was too soon for me to conduct the lead advance, but I was pleasantly surprised to be selected to conduct the security advance for the Hilton Hotel the staff chose for the trip. This particular hotel had a reputation in the Secret Service for being extremely difficult to secure due to its complex layout. It was commonly referred to as the "Upside-Down Hilton."

The hotel was built into the side of a mountain, and the entrance was located on the top floor and was labeled "L." The floors below it went up in number as the elevator descended. If you want to go down a floor from the third floor in the Trinidad Hilton, you must press the button for the fourth floor. Although this sounds simple, I often encountered confused guests in the elevators over the course of the two-week advance. The layout of each floor was confusing as well, and many of the emergency evacuation exits would have exposed the president to exterior portions of the building, a factor I deemed unacceptable and worked diligently to design my plan around.

As a general rule, I would never evacuate the president from one attack with unknown variables into another scenario with an unknown outcome. If we evacuate, I want to know exactly where we are going and have a purpose for doing it. Sometimes it is far better to stay and defend what you have rather than try to defend an area you're not sure you can tactically control.

The president's arrival in Trinidad was welcomed by the advance team, as many of the team members had become ill during the two-week advance. Surprisingly, given my history of contracting illnesses on foreign soil, I had managed to avoid any serious illness. The initial portion of the visit at the hotel went smoothly because, outside of sleeping, the president spent very little time there. Toward the end of the trip I was informed by Steve, the lead advance, that the president would hold a press conference on the hotel roof during the final hours of the visit and just prior to his departure from the country. I retreated to my hotel room to put together the security plan.

Hotel roofs are some of the most dangerous places from a security standpoint, and holding a press conference there with all of the potential dangers (e.g., sniper fire, high winds) was going to require some creativity. Complicating the situation was the rapid deterioration of my physical condition. After avoiding illness for nearly two weeks, I began to feel very ill, very quickly. Memories of the dengue fever episode still fresh in my mind, I became concerned. With just one more day left in the advance, I was determined to get through it and not become a burden to the team. I did not want to disappoint and worked late into the night, heavily medicated by the always-helpful doctors from the White House Medical Unit.

When I awoke in the morning, I could barely roll out of the hotel room bed. The idea of putting on a bullet-resistant vest, a wool suit, and a tie in the searing Caribbean heat made the physical pain that much more intense. I took the medication the White House doctor had given me and met with Steve in front of the president's suite and discussed the plan for the press conference. Steve was an intuitive and caring agent and could immediately see I was not well. I told him I could get through it and he responded by pulling my head close to his and saying, "It's the fourth quarter; don't come out of the game now."

I assured him I would complete the assignment and, although I was running a high fever and sweating profusely, I was comforted by the idea that the trip was just hours from ending. While heading up to the press conference with the president in the elevator, I felt the strange looks from the Secret Service, military, and White House staff as they noticed my pale color and heavy sweating against the backdrop of an artificial smile. Press conferences in foreign countries can run very long, and with each passing minute standing in the hot sun in a suit, wearing the bullet-resistant vest, and carrying nearly twenty pounds of equipment, I became increasingly worried that I might lose consciousness. The ramifications for such a public display of failure would have been devastating to me, and the fear kept me lucid. The feeling of relief when the president concluded his remarks gave me the rush of adrenaline I needed to hurriedly move him down one level via the stairs to the limo and see him off without incident.

The White House photographer, Pete, took an official White House photo of the moment the president entered the vehicle that shows me looking up and loudly asking a guest to close his hotel window. I was sent the picture and when I look at it, I clearly remember how terrible I felt.

Completing the Trinidad Hilton advance allowed me to check a box on my imaginary career "to-do" list. The Secret Service is a remarkable agency that imbues in its agents a loyalty to the mission that far outweighs financial reward. Imagine a private business asking its employees to take on a responsibility commensurate with securing the life of the president of the United States, to work ten to sixteen hours per day without a day off in a foreign country, where your life is constantly in danger, and to do it all for no additional compensation. This is the life of a PPD lead advance agent assigned to a foreign advance in a high-threat-level country. Yet despite these conditions, PPD agents clamor for the opportunity to be assigned a foreign advance, and the more dangerous the more rewarding. I credit the Secret Service, which, whether intentionally or accidentally, has created this culture where your credibility as an agent depends on your taking on increasing levels of responsibility and rewards those agents who complete the most difficult assignments. The rewards are not material but are largely based on group dynamics and social prestige within the detail. After checking the foreign hotel advance box, I was anxious to move on to lead advance work and was happy to be assigned my first position in Youngstown, Ohio, at a Caterpillar plant.

My first lead advance was what PPD agents called an "in and out," or a trip where the president was visiting only one location, was on the ground for a short period of time, and did not remain overnight. The visit was made even less complex by the fact that the entire advance team was able to drive to Youngstown from Washington, DC, avoiding travel logistics complications. In addition, the presidential staff made the choice to fly via Marine One directly to an open field just outside the site, which nearly eliminated any chance of a motorcade security threat. It was during this visit that I created a security approach I referred to as a "box within a box."

The advance team that was assigned to the visit was very talented, but we collectively had a difficult time agreeing on a cost-effective and practical method to secure an enormous Caterpillar plant to presidential security standards. The plant was a security nightmare and contained dangerous chemicals, potentially dangerous equipment, and hundreds of individual office spaces. After lengthy discussions about how to tackle this, I suggested we create a "box within a box." Using this approach, a security team can allocate scarce law-enforcement and military assets to prioritize and secure only the areas where the protectee will be physically present and designate the outlying areas for electronic and personnel-based surveillance. The site agent skillfully implemented the model using a series of hardened steel containers that created a nearly impenetrable room within the plant where the president could conduct his visit. The trip was successful and I have since written opinion pieces for different outlets describing how the "box within a box" approach can be applied to challenging security problems such as school security.

It was also on this trip that I had a life-altering conversation with an older, more experienced agent I considered a mentor. Ken and I had become quick friends on the PPD where he had been assigned as a supervisor, and his presence on the Youngstown trip was a bonus. Similar to Steve, the agent I worked with on the Trinidad trip, Ken always had sage advice to pass on, advice that was the result of life experience, work experience, and a keen instinct for when to talk and when to listen. Ken had been assigned to a number of high-profile assignments, including a lengthy stint on Capitol Hill in the office of a prominent senator, and his experiences had changed him, both for the better and the worse.

Although I loved my time with the Secret Service and would not have traded the rich experiences and deep, personal friendships with some of my fellow agents for anything, something was missing. Ken sensed my apprehension and, after a day of challenging advance work in Youngstown, I told him that I was thinking about leaving. I did not know for what at the time, but I told him that I felt I had to leave a dent in the world and was unsure if this was the avenue I was supposed to do it through. Ken was a deeply religious but not preachy gentleman, and he told me to pray on it and to look for spiritual guidance. He was clear that you must ask for help and that the answers would be obvious, but only if you have the guts to take the test. It was after this conversation that the idea of politics appeared on my conscious radar screen.

Moving from brief "in and out" visits to high-threat-level foreign advances is a leap in responsibility and stress, and the lead advances I conducted in the aftermath of the Ohio trip helped prepare me for the tasks ahead. After successfully completing lead advance assignments in Albuquerque, New Mexico; Newark, New Jersey; and Martha's Vineyard, Massachusetts, with minimal disruptions, our PPD operations section placed me on a list of lead advance agents qualified to conduct foreign advances. I traveled extensively as an agent both on and off of PPD and understood the complications of dealing with foreign governments. I was elated when I received notification that I was selected as the lead advance agent for President Obama's trip to Jakarta, Indonesia.

This complicated trip was fraught with difficulty from the moment it was announced, and I was honored to be selected considering all the variables involved. The first problem was the location. Indonesia is over ten thousand miles away from Washington, DC, and with a time difference of twelve hours, communicating with PPD operations from the field would be challenging. The second obstacle was the threat level within the country. The president "imports" an elevated threat level to locations he visits by nature of simply being there. Threats follow us wherever we go, but Indonesia needed no such assistance. They had a homegrown terrorist network in Jemaah Islamiyah, which had successfully planned and implemented a number of serious terrorist attacks, including the deadly Bali bombing in 2002 that killed and injured over two hundred people. The third problem I saw with the visit was not directly related to the security situation or the logistics but the politics. Indonesia was one of the president's childhood homes and there was going to be intense pressure from all the relevant players to ensure flawless planning and implementation. The president would surely notice mistakes on the visit that may have escaped detection on other trips, and the White House staff, the Secret Service, and the Indonesian military and law-enforcement personnel were well aware that this operation had to be perfect.

We arrived in Indonesia after a series of flights that would test the patience of even the most experienced traveler. After three flights, over twenty hours in the air, and with long layovers in between, we arrived at Halim Perdanakusuma Airport in Indonesia physically exhausted. We were short on time for the security advance given the many complications involved with the visit, and I told the team that we would have to get started shortly after arrival, which was sure to impose misery on an exhausted advance team. The White House staff advance, Carrie, was also aware of the importance of the visit and wanted to start as quickly as possible and she agreed with my decision. The relationship between the White House staff and the Secret Service is inherently adversarial given the conflicting missions, but I found Carrie willing to compromise and felt that she understood the dangerous environment. Carrie accommodated requests that under different circumstances would have likely resulted in a "war of phone calls," where she would call back to the White House chief of staff's office in Washington and I would call back to PPD operations warning them to expect a phone call from the chief of staff's office, a ridiculous but sometimes necessary game of political chess.

The initial meeting with the deputy chief of mission, the embassy staff, and the White House staff went very well, and I sensed that the Indonesians were firmly committed to ensuring a productive and safe trip for the president. The follow-up police meeting with the rest of the Secret Service advance team was an impressive show. The Indonesians had hundreds of law-enforcement and military personnel in attendance and ensured us that this was an "all hands on deck" effort. I was severely jet lagged, but took the stage and proudly introduced our team and explained our requirements to our hosts. The security services in Indonesia were the best they had to offer. They were taken from the elite Paspampres, a group of men chosen from the Indonesian military and assigned to secure the life of the Indonesian president, effectively their Secret Service.

At the time of our visit, the Paspampres were under the charge of a physically impressive figure with a booming voice, General Marciano Norman, the current head of the Indonesian State Intelligence Agency. Norman was close with Indonesian president Susilo Bambang Yudhoyono (recall my lesson from Panama that in some countries "those who have the guns have the power"), and maintaining a good relationship with him was going to be central to the success of the mission, whereas one wrong calculation with Norman and the success of the visit was in danger. There was very little Norman could not fix if we needed him to, and when Norman spoke it was clear he was speaking on behalf of the Indonesian president. My relationship with Norman, although delicate, helped clear a number of bureaucratic hurdles, which always impacted the degree of progress on any foreign advance. I learned quickly to filter my requests in stages, preparing him slowly for what was sure to be an unprecedented request for intelligence assets, equipment, manpower, and traffic control.

The threat of terrorism and the personal safety of the team was a constant concern for me during the advance. The president receives Secret Service protection, but the Secret Service is not entitled to the same luxury. Force protection became a priority for me, and I met daily with representatives from the Jakarta Shangri-La to see what they were doing to prevent another bombing of the type that occurred at the JW Marriott in South Jakarta in 2003. I could not explain to the family of a fellow Secret Service agent that I lost him or her to an attack because we were so focused on the president's security that we let our own lapse.

The security in the hotel was under the watch of an American expat who was experienced in modern security methodology. He assured me that the team would be safe in his hotel, and I trusted him. Learning to quickly evaluate and discriminate between the "talkers" and the "doers" was a skill I had refined and I trusted that he was a "doer." The security operation I planned was to be massive in size and incomparable in its scale and scope. Many of the sites the president would visit were outdoors, including one that posed especially challenging issues. Kalibata Cemetery is a solemn place dedicated to Indonesian's military heroes, but each time I visited with the White House staff and the Indonesian security team I uncovered a new security nightmare. The president would have an exposed walk to a monument with no easy evacuation route and it was surrounded by high ground, a sniper's dream. Combined with a long-distance motorcade route from the hotel, this site was going to require a detailed plan and substantial manpower before we could even entertain the idea of visiting there.

After about a week of planning and co-opting nearly every Indonesian military and law-enforcement official available, to the chagrin of my Indonesian counterparts, I was informed that the Indonesian visit might not happen. Carrie told me that the negotiations regarding the Patient Protection and Affordable Care Act, otherwise known as "Obamacare," might prevent the president from traveling and the trip would be rescheduled.

I was stunned by the news, considering the volume of work already dedicated to the visit by all the involved parties. The thought of traveling to the opposite side of the globe, working day and night to ensure the visit went smoothly, and now having it cancelled was devastating. I anxiously awaited notification but suspected that the decision had already been made in the White House. My suspicions were confirmed in the hotel workroom, where I had nearly lived for the week prior, when I turned on the Fox News Channel and heard White House Press Secretary Robert Gibbs apologize to his international hosts and declare that the president would be cancelling his overseas visits to focus on the negotiations over Obamacare. Although it was morning in Washington when the announcement was made official, it was late at night in Indonesia given the twelve-hour time difference.

I was frustrated that the White House staff on the ground in Indonesia had not informed me sooner. International negotiations and diplomacy are always delicate, and I was sure that General Norman would suspect that I had kept this information from him and that the White House staff in Indonesia had known in advance about the cancellation. I immediately picked up the closest phone in an effort to prevent Norman from learning about the cancellation on the news as well and quickly dialed his assistant Frega's number. I profusely apologized to Frega and thanked him for his dedication to ensuring a safe visit. Frega was a decent man and said he understood and assured me that there would be no hard feelings with Norman.

Along with the disappointed advance team, I flew the ten thousand miles home upset that I missed a rare opportunity to conquer the PPD's most difficult task, a foreign security advance in a dangerous corner of the world.

12

MISSILE TREATIES AND THE RETURN TO INDONESIA

AFTER MAKING THE LONG JOURNEY home from Indonesia, profoundly disappointed at the wasted effort put in by me and the team, I decided to use some of my accrued vacation time to spend time with Paula and our daughter, Isabel.

Since being designated a lead advance agent, I had been traveling domestically and on foreign soil for months and desperately needed some time with my family. My young daughter noticed how much I was gone and when I returned home from Indonesia, she innocently asked me, "Daddy, are you allowed to sleep here tonight?"

She had assumed that my wife and I had separated. Hearing that was emotionally devastating. I had missed so many birthdays and holidays and those are moments that once lost, can never be retrieved. Paula was understanding, but she was beginning to grow frustrated as well. Excited about the time off from the daily rigor, I drove into PPD operations to drop off the secure phones and diplomatic passports assigned to the Indonesia advance team and planned on leaving the office quickly to get home and start my vacation. Unfortunately, this was not to be.

When I walked into the White House complex, Marlon, the supervisor in the operations section, asked me if I was ready to go out again. Confused, I asked him what he meant. He told me that the White House was in the end stages of negotiations regarding the START II treaty, and depending on the results of the negotiations, the president might travel to Prague to sign the treaty with Russian president Dmitry Medvedev.

With my interest in foreign policy at its peak, I was following the treaty negotiations closely but strictly out of personal interest; I had no intention of actually becoming part of the story. It never occurred to me that there would be personal ramifications for me at the end of the negotiations. Marlon was being briefed on the status of the negotiations on an hourly basis, and he informed me that PPD management wanted me to conduct the foreign advance in Prague and that I should hold onto my passport and the phones.

The drive home from the White House that day was difficult. I was jet-lagged from the Indonesia trip, and I knew telling Paula that I would have to leave again would be painful for both of us. Although we lived together, we rarely saw one another anymore and her words to me when we were dating and I was transferred from the New York field office to the training center in Maryland were fresh in my mind: *"amor de lejos es amor de pendejos"* or "love from afar is love for fools."

Unfortunately, when PPD management "asks" you to take on a difficult assignment, they are really not asking. It is expected that you will agree to it without complaint, as even the perception of whining or complaining about assignments can end a career. Before I made it through the garage door to my house, Marlon called and said the trip to Prague was a go and that I should be prepared for an abbreviated advance schedule. I asked him to allow me to pick my advance team due to the short time

I was going to have to secure the visit and sort out the security accommodations we were going to have to make to the Russians, who were also in Prague preparing for their president's security. The Russians, from my experience, were skilled negotiators.

I selected the most talented advance team I could and the following day we embarked on our trip to Prague. As I left, I could see that Paula was extremely upset. But she saw the fatigue in my face and did not want to contribute any further to my growing frustration with the circumstances, so she wished me well.

My team had one week in Prague to do what was at least two weeks' worth of work, so we had to work efficiently to keep to our compressed timeline. I was facing long days and nights ahead and was nearing the point of complete exhaustion due to the chaos the constant changing of time zones was having on my internal clock. I survived on strong coffee, and after my initial meeting with the Czech law-enforcement and security personnel, I was confident we could complete the mission successfully.

The Czech security services were skilled operators and it was clear that they knew what needed to be done in a short period of time. Despite the physical and emotional fatigue, the team and I kept a rigorous work schedule and put together a thorough plan. Having been afforded the opportunity by Marlon to personally select my own advance team for the visit had paid dividends in this rushed operation. The men and women I selected were no-nonsense types who were known to work long hours and require little to no supervision. I did not have the time on the visit to micromanage anyone's individual assignment and did not need to as they performed admirably.

After a series of intense negotiations with the Russian diplomatic entourage and security personnel over everything from the locations of our snipers to whether the presidents would be seated or standing, I proudly witnessed the signing of the treaty by both presidents. I was relieved to complete the operation without incident and was desperate to get back home to my family. But at the end of the visit I suspected my plans to get home, incredibly, might be sidetracked again when Polish president Lech Kaczynski was killed in a plane crash on April 10, 2010. Poland was within driving distance of the Czech Republic and I knew the United States was going to send a representative, and it was likely to be the president.

Already past the point of fatigue, I hoped that PPD operations would find someone else to conduct the advance should the president attend. My concerns were eliminated by the eruption of a volcano in Iceland and the associated atmospheric ash, which made the flight to Poland too dangerous. The advance team and I quickly closed down the work area in the hotel, shredded all documents, and rushed to the airport to escape the ash and return to the US. We arrived home safely but, oddly, it would not be my last experience attempting to escape volcanic ash in a hurry to get home.

After spending some time at home with my family and staying busy with advance work within the United States, I began to grow concerned over the state of the country and my role in it. I saw a journey down an economic path our government had tried before with disastrous results, and as a result my academic interest in economics turned into a passion. I spent every spare moment I could find, whether on planes or during lunch, reading voluminous amounts of material on Austrian School economic theory. It fueled in me what was quickly becoming a fiery passion for political engagement. It appeared that the only thing that could keep me from politics was an advance assignment, but due to my recent work in Prague and Indonesia I didn't expect another big assignment in the immediate future. My assumptions about my workload could not have been more incongruous with what was to come.

In June of 2010, I received a phone call from PPD operations asking me how I felt about Indonesia. Confused, I responded that I had a wonderful time there and was disappointed that the visit was cancelled. I was told that the visit was now officially back on and that PPD management wanted me to return to Indonesia to repeat the advance based on my prior experience there. I knew this would cause some consternation with the PPD lead advance agents because these important assignments were becoming increasingly more difficult to come by, given the president's limited travel schedule with the Obamacare negotiations and the now-erupting BP oil spill crisis.

I agreed to do the advance and travel as soon as possible. When I told Paula what was happening she was understandably apprehensive, believing that we were tempting fate by returning to a high-threat zone with the same presidential schedule. I could not disagree with her, but I felt we could secure the visit and had no desire to see someone else get hurt if I chose to pass on the assignment. After convincing Paula that I would be fine, I began the long journey back to Indonesia. Paula was again visibly upset and I empathized with her. The travel was now becoming so intense that sleeping in my own bed was an anomaly. When we landed in Hong Kong after the second leg of our long journey, I turned on the satellite phone to call Paula and tell her we were fine. Noticing I had a message on it to call PPD operations, I turned to one of the advance team members and said, half jokingly, "Can you imagine how upset the Indonesians would be if this trip is cancelled again?"

When I called operations they said, "You are not going to believe this, but the trip is cancelled."

I was stunned. This was now the second time we had cancelled, and I knew the amount of diplomatic currency that had already been spent on the trip. Personally, it was going to be difficult to salvage any credibility with General Norman in Indonesia. He already allocated thousands of man-hours to this and now I would have to call Frega and tell him the trip was cancelled again.

As it turns out, the BP oil spill in the Gulf of Mexico had grown into a political embarrassment for President Obama as the spewing gash at the bottom of the ocean was causing a media frenzy. The president could not leave the country until there was some action on this growing environmental disaster. I dreaded calling Frega, but in his always-dignified manner he assured me it was "no problem," although I knew it was. We had cancelled on him twice, and pretending that our credibility was intact was a useless exercise. I apologized profusely, and with the entire advance team, I rushed to book yet another flight home.

13

OIL SPILLS, INDONESIA AGAIN, AND MAKING A WAR ZONE "SAFE"

ARRIVING HOME AFTER THE SECOND CANCELLATION of the Indonesia trip, I resolved to myself that my time on the detail was coming to an end and the trip was just not meant to happen. I hated that we worked tirelessly on a plan that would never be implemented and the international law-enforcement relationships between us and the Indonesians were left to wither.

I was not home for more than a few hours when PPD operations called me about assisting another agent during his first lead advance assignment. The agent was Tim, my good friend from our time together at the training center and the PPD transportation section. I was honored to do it and, although Paula was upset at my having to leave again, she and Tim were friends, and she understood what needed to be done. Tim and I were sent to Dauphin Island, Alabama, with the president to search for signs of the oil spill. It appeared that the White House staff was desperate to have the president appear as if he were "doing something" and wanted some photo ops of him on an oily beach looking concerned. The public generally sees through this type of thing, but every presidential administration I worked for used this strategy regardless of how obviously orchestrated it appears.

We met the staff on Dauphin Island and got started quickly getting to know the area. It was obvious in a short amount of time that there did not appear to be significant damage to the beachfront. The White House staff could not have the president on a relatively clean beach giving statements to the press about the devastation. In presidential politics this is a "no-go."

After a few days of looking and finding only small tar balls, the staff decided that it would be better to put the president on a boat and to ensure the press shots were of him looking into the ocean. It was an unusual request and the Secret Service, in general, prefers to avoid open ocean adventures with the president. But Tim was a skilled agent and he put together a very workable plan, although he ruffled some staff feathers in the process. Tim had no time for weakness or indecision and had no problem letting the White House staff know. This made him a hero to the advance team but a foe to the staff. Despite the personal disagreements, the visit went smoothly, with no unusual issues, and I took pages of mental notes on what was becoming a growing frustration with political leaders, their spin machines, and what seemed to me to be a premium placed on the style and not the substance of leadership.

After the successful completion of our Dauphin Island advance, I became one of a few agents that operations would select on a regular basis to serve as a "lead advisor." These were cherished assignments because the energy was high but the workload was dramatically reduced. The lead advance agent would rely on me for assistance but generally did most of the work himself. I figured that my last few months on the detail would be uneventful and that the advisor role was my last act on the PPD. I was scheduled to leave the PPD in December and it was now the end of

October, and I looked forward to the possibility of a nine-to-five workday in my next assignment. Life back in a field office after PPD was generally easier. Looking to avoid the devastating Washington, DC, traffic I requested the Baltimore field office. This was a difficult assignment to get because the office was small and openings were rare, but I was confident that the PPD would do their best to help facilitate the transfer.

My optimistic outlook quickly faded when I began to hear whispers within the detail that the Indonesia trip was being discussed again among the White House staff. Paula would certainly not accept my traveling to Indonesia for a third potential presidential visit with a similar schedule. The dangers would now be magnified because any group looking to do harm to the president would have had months to plan. Although no one from PPD operations confirmed any plans with me, I was sure I was going to be asked to return again. I began to slowly prepare Paula for the eventual phone call from operations, and only days later I found myself, now for a third time, on the long flight back to Indonesia.

I reunited with Frega, the representative for General Norman, and made a point to apologize for all of the confusion. Frega was always a gentleman and once again pretended not to mind, although I knew it was bothering him. The advance work was made easier logistically since I was already familiar with the country and many of our Indonesian military and police counterparts. The security planning, however, was going to be more difficult, as it was no mystery among the Indonesians and their press corps where the president intended to visit while in the country.

Dealing with the homegrown threat of terrorism and trying to make a well-known itinerary secure was difficult, but the new White House staff lead, Dave, who had replaced the now-departed Carrie, was willing to work with us. I insisted on deception in all aspects of the plan and was determined to never use the same motorcade route, vehicle lineup, or entrance to any location twice. When the team and I looked at all the variables, we felt that unpredictability would be our greatest asset and injected deception and randomness to our security plans whenever possible.

The seemingly endless string of bad luck with this trip was not over. As we approached the arrival date, Indonesia's Mount Merapi began to spew volcanic ash. This was a grave concern for the Air Force One advance team on the ground. They were worried that the ash could clog the engines of Air Force One and potentially take the plane down. Indonesia and Washington, DC, were twelve hours apart on the clock, and the briefings between the senior White House staff, the White House Military Office, PPD management, and me were on their time, not mine. Information changed hourly and the phone rang with each new update, many times at two and three o'clock in the morning Indonesian local time.

The lack of sleep was taking its toll and I was having a difficult time staying awake during the day. The decision to make the trip or not was now in the hands of the White House Military Office and its atmospheric forecasters. To my surprise, instead of cancelling again, the decision was made to cut the visit short by one day but to still make the journey from India, the president's first stop on his itinerary.

The India portion of the trip was a "disaster," according to some friends of mine who were detailed there, and the PPD management was in no mood for more mishaps. The Indian security force assigned to the visit had reneged on deals made during the advance and they openly defied the Secret Service advance team's wishes, creating an embarrassing situation for both the Secret Service and the staff. Patience wore thin, and I knew our visit had to be flawless.

The fun began when a security representative from the hotel where the president would be staying rushed toward me with a concerned look on his face and a picture in his hand. He stated that a man had checked into multiple rooms in the hotel using different names and moved back and forth between these rooms before leaving the hotel. The Indonesians confirmed for us that the man had affiliations with a number of groups that were a very serious concern for me and the intelligence agents on the ground.

The stress was magnified under the circumstances and decisions were required very quickly, as Air Force One was in the air from India and headed to us in Indonesia. I could not bring the president to the hotel until I was absolutely sure that it was clear of threats. The explosives sweep had turned up nothing and had taken hours to complete due to the complexity of the hotel layout, and we did not have hours to redo the sweep. I asked the team to resweep and search the rooms the man had checked into. At the same time I asked the hotel security team to ensure that the man was questioned if he attempted to reenter the hotel.

When the sweep came back with negative results, I was slightly relieved but I began to wonder if all the bad luck surrounding this trip was a sign that it was doomed. Suffering from the chronic lack of sleep and feeling extremely uncomfortable wearing suffocating clothing in the near-hundred-degree heat, I prepared our motorcade and departed for the airport to finally pick up the president.

The Indonesia trip, now officially cut short due to the ash plumes from the erupting volcano, was proceeding along without incident as we moved from the airport to the hotel and on to the Indonesian presidential palace. The security plan we designed was working perfectly, but the ash plumes were getting thicker and the White House Military Office was growing increasingly concerned. The following morning I met with the PPD advance team and the supervisors assigned to the visit and was informed that in order to cut the visit by a few more hours, we were cancelling the last scheduled stop and going directly from a speech at a local university to the airport.

It was becoming a race against time to beat the erupting volcano and the advancing ash plume. Our first stop of the day at Istiqlal Mosque was rushed as we hurried along to the speech site. The president received a hero's welcome at the university despite the shortened schedule. We still had not located the suspicious man at the hotel, and with the advancing ash plume, I was content to see the president leave the country earlier than expected. Coordinating the logistics of the early departure was made slightly more complicated because the president was not returning to the United States but was flying directly to South Korea, and they were not ready to receive him.

I contacted Colin, the lead advance in South Korea, and told him that he would have to meet with the South Koreans to adjust the schedule. Meanwhile, I quietly prayed during the motorcade from the university to the airport that the security plan would hold and we would get the president off the ground without incident. The stress was mounting and, combined with oppressive fatigue and the searing Indonesian heat, I feared the worst. Between the suspicious hotel guest, the indigenous threats I dealt with daily, and the ash cloud that threatened to strand the president in Indonesia if we fell even minutes behind schedule, I was constantly on the cell phone with new requests for the team.

Fortunately, the advance team assigned to the visit was tier one and they superseded expectations each and every time I called them with a

Pennsylvania Avenue during President Obama's first inauguration in January 2009.

In Port of Spain, Trinidad, for the Summit of the Americas on April 2009 taken immediately after President Obama concluded the press conference at the Hilton Trinidad. *Photo courtesy White House photographer Pete Souza*

In the Oval Office in January 2011, subsequent to my departure from the Presidential Protective Division. *Photo courtesy White House photographer Lawrence Jackson*

Interviewing with NBC at the Republican National Convention in Tampa, Florida, in August 2012. We were discussing the irony of walking through metal detectors that I had used in designing security plans as an agent. *Photo courtesy Karla Graham*

Interviewing with Brian Todd of CNN in June 2011, in front of the White House I used to protect, after announcing my candidacy for the US Senate. *Photo courtesy Karla Graham*

At Capitol Hill, taken April 15, 2013, just hours before the bombing at the Boston Marathon. I was giving a speech at a FreedomWorks rally in Washington, DC. *Photo courtesy O.P. Ditch*

In Kent County, Maryland, taken shortly after my Republican primary victory. It was the first time my opponent, Sen. Ben Cardin, and I met. *Photo courtesy Dan Divilio*

Pennsylvania Avenue during President Obama's 2009 Inauguration. *Photo by Mary F. Calvert* / The Washington Times. *Copyright © 2009 The Washington Times LLC. This reprint does not constitute or imply any endorsement or sponsorship of any product, service, company or organization.*

White House South Grounds during an NCAA sports recognition event. *Photo by AFP / Getty Images*

TSTC Waco Airport in Waco, Texas, at the conclusion of my first Presidential Protective Division advance assignment.

John F. Kennedy International Airport in Queens, NY, during the 2008 United Nations General Assembly in the final months of the George W. Bush administration. *Photo by AFP / Getty Images*

The 2008 White House Christmas party. *Official White House photo*

change or new request. After multiple trips and thousands of man-hours dedicated to an airtight security plan, I feared that a random mishap at the last minute could ruin what was left of the goodwill the team and I built with the Indonesians. During my trip to Paris with President Bush, a dog had rushed into the street and nearly caused an accident with the presidential limo, so I was keenly aware of the potential for a random disaster on a moment's notice. At my request the motorcade drove quickly, and the staff moved the president briskly through a few thank-yous to local dignitaries. Despite the many complications, Air Force One was in the air minutes later. The relief and elation I felt was indescribable as the nearly yearlong advance operation finally came to an end.

But the sense of relief was short-lived. Before we made it back to the hotel, I received a phone call from one of the logistics agents at the airport. All of the support personnel in Indonesia to help implement the security plan were being told that they might be stranded due to the atmospheric ash and the military's inability to fly us out. This was both a logistics and security nightmare for me. I intentionally placed all our personnel in hotels with layered security plans and within a short distance of our command center in the event of an emergency, and none of these locations had any rooms available. I feared that it would become widely known that the American security team was stranded in Jakarta and that we would become an appetizing target for the local terrorist groups.

I called operations and asked for permission to bypass financial restrictions on the cost of flights home as the only alternative. Although the available flight plans involved convoluted layovers, the logistics team managed to find flights home for most of the stranded personnel. The remaining staff were forced to stay on cots in rooms we had at the Shangri-La. It was not ideal, but I was sure it was secure. Eventually, we all made the trip home safely, some flying thousands of miles in the wrong direction just to get out of the country to a connecting flight.

Having now successfully "checked the box" on designing and implementing a complete foreign security advance plan in both Prague and Jakarta, and having my request for vacation time approved, I was sure I had seen my last assignment as an agent on the PPD.

On my second day of vacation I was in my basement exercising, trying to sweat out the illness I had returned from Indonesia with, when my phone rang. On the other end was Vic, the second in command among PPD management, and he asked me if I could see him tomorrow at his office in the White House. I knew not to ask a lot of questions and simply said yes, but was perplexed as to what he could want to discuss. Ideas began to filter through my mind. I wondered if something had happened in Indonesia that I had not been made aware of.

The following day, I drove to the White House hoping that the unusual request to meet Vic in his office during my vacation was not the result of something I had done wrong. Vic and I developed a solid working relationship during my tenure on the PPD and when I sat down in his office, he engaged in some brief small talk. Then he quickly cut to the chase and asked me if I would be willing to go out again.

I couldn't believe what I was hearing, I had vacation time already approved and was scheduled to leave the detail in just one week for my new assignment in Baltimore. Vic told me that the president was planning to visit Afghanistan and that the trip was to be kept "dark" until we landed on the ground at Bagram Airfield. He asked me to conduct the advance and said I would have to leave the next morning. He assured me that he would notify the Baltimore field office that I was sick and that my transfer there would be delayed. I accepted the assignment and began to wonder how I was going to explain this to Paula yet again.

Paula and I had been together long enough where she could predict with incredible accuracy what I was going to tell her. I was bound to not to disclose the visit, even to Paula, so I told her I had an "assignment" and that I had to fly out of the country immediately. She cried and asked me to turn it down, clearly emotionally drained by the entire PPD experience. She felt that she had married me, not the Secret Service, yet they had taken me away from her. She was not an overly superstitious person, but she believed that after I had made it safely back from Indonesia that we had tempted fate, and she desperately wanted to avoid any other scenario where I could be in harm's way. She was also savvy enough to know that I was not headed to a luxury resort given the top secret nature of the visit. I did my best to console her and assured her that this was the last trip, that it was all over after this, but unfortunately she had heard this all before. My daughter Isabel was also devastated that I was going to be overseas, because it was my birthday and she had planned something special.

I pondered how much more of this I could take. It was not the workload but the emotional toll it was taking on my family that was growing intolerable. I took solace in the fact that this was surely the last lead advance in a "hot zone" I would ever do and that if I made it back, it was finally over.

We landed at Bagram Airfield on a cold December afternoon, having traveled under an umbrella of secrecy from Joint Base Andrews in Maryland. The base in Afghanistan was not informed of the exact reason for our assignment but was told to provide support for a visit by a "dignitary."

I was honored to be working with our fighting men and women. Having lost my Uncle Gregory in Vietnam, I always revered men and women willing to selflessly forfeit their lives for the freedom of others. The men and women at Bagram did not disappoint; they worked tirelessly with us to ensure a "safe" war zone. When talking to the soldiers, I found it incredible how many were proud to be there but felt unsure of achieving the mission's long-term goals. I took every opportunity to speak with the soldiers I was working with, and I listened with rapt attention as they described their experiences and the stories of soldiers who had been wounded, maimed, or killed in action. Touring the hospital at the airfield was devastating. I saw the horrifying injuries as a result of improvised explosives, and the delicate care given to our to our enemies as well as to our men. The trip to Afghanistan permanently changed my view of our country's involvement in that war. It may be clichéd to say, but it was a life-changing experience.

Planning and implementing a security advance in an active war zone is a challenge few Secret Service agents have experienced. Preparing for incoming mortar fire, the very real danger of Air Force One being shot out of the sky, and the threat of an organized attack with heavy weapons by a determined quasi-military unit are not common threats within the United States, but they were daily occurrences in Afghanistan.

A few days into the trip, I met with General David Petraeus, the commander of the International Security Assistance Force, in downtown Kabul after flying from Bagram in the back of a war-torn C-130 cargo plane. Our meeting with the general was pleasant. I found him to be very receptive to our ideas and I was honored that, given his experience in the country, he was eager to hear and adapt my ideas on how we could ensure the safety of the president in this unique situation. We discussed some options on transport for the president should he decide to make the trip to Kabul, and although the general assured me that transportation could be secured, I was hesitant to approve it. This became a contentious issue, with widely varying opinions on the matter. General Petraeus felt it could be done, but some of his subordinates felt otherwise and the intelligence operators on the ground strongly advised against it. They believed once it was discovered that we were there, we would be shot out of the sky by rocket-propelled grenade fire upon departure from Kabul. I deeply trusted the intelligence team on the ground. They worked under extremely dangerous conditions and, sadly, the facility where I met with them was attacked with heavy weapons two years later and two heroes were lost.

The decision to let the president fly to Kabul from Bagram was going to be a defining moment for me. After a meeting with Ambassador Karl Eikenberry at our embassy in Kabul, I remained skeptical that the trip could be secured. I knew we could effectively ensure the security of the airfield at Bagram, but downtown Kabul was like nothing I had ever seen. It appeared that time had forgotten portions of the city, and law and order were non-existent. We traveled with heavily armed teams and did not leave the US facility without heavily armored vests and in windowless armored vans.

Every location we visited was a security nightmare. There was no practical way to secure a group of city blocks that consisted of hollowed-out buildings and mazes of empty, crumbling stairwells. Securing the area would require potentially thousands of soldiers. The president of the United States is not simply a man—he is the singular, living embodiment of an entire branch of government, and any potential threat to his security must be completely mitigated. Our military partners in country had a remarkable "can do" attitude and their sense of duty was admirable, but I was unsure we could secure the visit to Kabul. This all came to a boil during a secure video teleconference call between me, my intelligence counterparts on the ground in Afghanistan, and the Situation Room in the White House.

After the Czech Republic and Indonesia, I was accustomed to being put on the spot by the White House staff, and this time I was forced to ask for more time. In the event they decided to override my recommendation to not take the president to Kabul, I began to design a plan to lock down the city. I never before requested the level of support that I needed for this operation and was uncomfortable that involving so many military personnel whom I had not worked with before would be distracting from their war mission. Regardless, we moved forward with the plan.

The hours prior to the president's arrival at Bagram Airfield were tense. A sandstorm made landing conditions for Air Force One treacherous, but had the positive side effect of eliminating the possibility of taking the helicopter trip to Kabul. After conferring with the White House military aide assigned to the visit, we decided to cancel the Kabul leg of the trip since the sandstorm conditions made the flight extremely dangerous. It did not escape me that all of the contentious negotiating regarding the danger of the Kabul visit was rendered meaningless due to the fortuitous intervention of Mother Nature.

I was relieved by this development, but I still needed reassurance from the White House military aide that Air Force One could safely land at the airfield, given the rapidly deteriorating conditions. The Air Force One advance team advised that it was going to be a tough landing but it could be done safely. Satisfied, but not content with his answer, I moved on to the next issue requiring immediate attention: the Secret Service advance agents who remained in Kabul to handle that portion of the visit were stranded there due to the sandstorm.

As I walked around the temporary command center trying to think through my options, I was informed that the president's staff was adding an event to the itinerary, now that some time had been freed up due to the cancellation of the Kabul visit. The president was going to meet with a group of soldiers in a vehicle bay and I needed to inspect the room. Upon entering, I saw a group of somber-looking soldiers and casually asked why they were meeting with the president. What I heard changed me forever. The ranking officer in the group said, "Because there were more of us last night."

He explained that during a patrol, their Afghan guide turned on them and shot multiple members of the group. The story was hard to fathom. It was stunning to hear firsthand how, in an attempt to free a country from the tyrannical grip of a savage group of Taliban cowards worshipping a philosophy of destruction and death, our men were killed by the beneficiaries of our goodwill. I was proud that these heroes would receive their moment with the president, but it again made me question every-thing I believed about this war. Somewhere, mothers, fathers, wives, and husbands were being asked to forfeit a future of endless possibilities with their sons, daughters, husbands, and wives in exchange for a cause many of those we fought for not only did not understand, but violently resented.

Watching Air Force One make a treacherous landing at Bagram in a sandstorm was an incredible sight and was the first sign the personnel on the airfield received that the "dignitary" they had been expecting was indeed the president. The visual contrast of the bold blue and white paint of Air Force One descending against the backdrop of the Afghan mountains in the dark desert night created a vision resembling a polished diamond against a deep, jet-black background. As the White House press pool feverishly snapped photos, the story was released and immediately filtered through the cable news channels.

My wife e-mailed me, finally realizing what my cryptic mission had been. Her messages were frantic as she was understandably concerned about my safety. The scene was one of controlled chaos and the lack of light on the airfield made it difficult to see anything outside of the camera flashes from the White House press pool photographers. We had to keep the lighting low to avoid being a target for enemy mortar fire so, to keep the president from tripping on the runway, I took out my flashlight to light his path.

The first stop was the troop rally and, although it was late at night local time, the reception by those in attendance was very warm. We worked at a distance from the president as he patiently shook every hand in the crowd, taking over an hour to greet every soldier. As the time passed, I grew more concerned about our security situation. I knew that our enemies were now aware that the president was on the ground, and with every minute the danger grew. I was also receiving minute-by-minute briefs on the status of our stranded personnel in Kabul. We desperately needed them to get in the air and on their way to Bagram.

My next stop with the president was the base hospital, where he would award Purple Hearts to the wounded heroes in the facility. I kept my distance from the president as he spoke with the soldiers out of respect for their privacy, and I saw the soldiers' faces light up as he spent time with each one. After five years on the PPD I felt ready to move on, but it was moments like these that always reignited my passion for my work.

As the night wore on, the exhaustion started to catch up with me. It was a huge relief to get the phone call from the Kabul team telling me that a brief window had opened and, although it was risky, they were able to fly and would land at Bagram with just enough time to make the flight home. The meeting with the soldiers was taking a while and I knew we had several hours ahead before the mission was complete. The final logistics were put in place. Air Force One would take off without runway lights to avoid being hit by mortar fire, but the lights would be activated for the support plane carrying me and my team. Therefore, to reduce our risk of being taken down by mortars, we had to take off immediately after Air Force One. To expedite the departure, I asked all the support personnel we could spare without sacrificing security to board the plane.

As the president finished his visit, I ensured he would say his final words while inside the hangar and not exposed on the runway. After this last meeting we would be finished with the visit, but not without a brief moment of unintended humor. President Obama was scheduled to meet with a small group of military officials and a Delta Force operator who was patiently standing outside the meeting room with all his equipment on, including his weapons. I was approached by a staff member who asked me if I wouldn't mind telling the Delta Force operator to relinquish his weapons before entering the room. Tired and in no mood for stupidity, I laughed loudly at this ridiculous request given that we had used every armed military unit on the base to help us secure the president and now he wanted me to ask an elite member of one of the finest military units the world has ever seen to drop his weapon. This brief interaction was a microcosm of the insulated, out-of-touch world some of the Washington, DC, cocktail party crowd operate in. One brief look into the Delta Force operator's eyes was enough to tell his story, a story that never has a happy ending but always has a hero as its subject.

After the meeting, we hurriedly loaded the president and his team onto the plane and within a few short minutes it was traveling down the dark runway and into the air. There was no time for any sigh of relief as the runway lights were turned on and we were now in very real danger if the support plane was targeted for attack. I jogged over to the plane, thanked my military counterparts, took a head count—and to my dismay I saw we were missing one of our military support personnel.

Minutes felt like hours as I called him over and over. After ten minutes I began to grow very concerned and the team on the plane began to worry as well. We could not stay much longer with the runway illuminated like a bright target for the enemy. It was then that I saw headlights and a military vehicle driving toward me. Leaping out of the vehicle as it was still moving, our lost team member appeared and with no time for questions, he boarded the plane and I told the pilot to go. It was the fastest I had ever seen a plane take off, and we were safely on our way home.

Finally, my five-year journey on the PPD had come to a close.

14

MEDIA SPIN VS. SECURITY REALITY

ADISTURBING MEDIA NARRATIVE began shortly after President Obama's inauguration that reflected poorly on the American people yet was entirely inaccurate. Despite any hard evidence, cable news outlets and prominent bloggers initiated a national conversation when they began speculating that President Obama had been receiving an unprecedented number of threats due to his race. What started in the editorial and opinion-based outlets soon became a mainstream media meme when a book about the Secret Service was released in 2009 that quoted an inside source as stating that threats to the new president were up nearly 400 percent. This misleading and inaccurate statistic disregards a number of trends I witnessed firsthand while working in the Protective Intelligence Unit in the New York field office and while assigned to the PPD.

During my twelve-year tenure with the Secret Service, the volume of reported threats to our designated protectees increased. That is not in dispute. However, there is a clear difference between reported threats and an increased general threat level. The exponential growth in social media platforms and mobile communication created an environment where casual threats could be easily made and just as easily reported. Threats, both veiled and direct, made in bars or between friends and relatives historically were only occasionally reported to the Secret Service and only investigated when someone who had actually witnessed or heard the threat reported the person making the threat. This changed with the advent of social media and the growth in e-mail communications. Threats via e-mail could now be easily forwarded on and social media postings that contained threats could be shared and "retweeted," enabling any concerned person reading the threat to initiate a Secret Service investigation. The stories of the "overwhelming" threat level to President Obama ignored the simple facts that the Secret Service does not publicly disclose its statistics on threats to the president and that the general threat level to President Obama was relatively consistent with historical trends.

In my experience, the social media factor alone is primarily responsible for the growth in threat reporting, yet in spite of this, the media firestorm surrounding the report of a 400 percent increase in threats and an "overwhelming" threat level because of the president's race grew until it was finally refuted months later in congressional testimony by Secret Service director Mark Sullivan. I had never witnessed such a blatant misuse of data attributed to anonymous sources to indict a nation and broadly claim that racism was driving a desire to harm the president. Anyone who questions a media bias need look no further than the irresponsible, headline-grabbing reports on this particular story to confirm that it exists.

The growth in threat reporting will likely continue as increasing numbers of people join social media networks. The Secret Service cannot ignore any threat regardless of its absurdity, and this is creating a strain on resources. Many within the agency feel strongly that the Secret Service should maintain its role as a lead agency in the investigation of financial crimes, and others feel that it should focus more on dignitary protection. Maintaining a dual mission as a protection agency and an investigative agency is going to become increasingly difficult in the future as threat reporting continues to grow, and it will be harder to defend in an atmosphere of constrained financial resources.

The Secret Service, along with a number of other federal law-enforcement agencies, could solve the majority of its manpower issues by agreeing to forfeit duplicative, redundant investigative mandates already filled by other federal agencies. The FBI has the capacity to absorb the Secret Service's computer crimes division and a significant portion of its financial crimes investigations. Counterfeiting could be turned over to underused federal investigators in the Treasury Department. These simple adjustments would free thousands of agents to focus exclusively on protection and threat assessment and investigation. It is understandable that this is not what the upper echelons of power within these agencies wish to hear, but I am confident that they quietly know it to be true.

As I've said already in this book, with big, bureaucratic government come big, bureaucratic consequences, and one of those consequences is that the bureaucracy's primary reason for existence over time becomes to protect itself. The reason often cited by Secret Service headquarters representatives for holding on to the investigative mission is that conducting federal criminal investigations ensures a higher quality of protection agent. In my experience this claim is not based on fact. It seems that many of the headquarters staff who continue to erroneously make this claim are also lobbying for retirement positions within financial institutions where they have supervised investigations, and they are reluctant to lose a bargaining chip.

The Secret Service criminal investigators I have worked with are some of the finest in the world, but no amount of spin is going to make two plus two equal five. In a future of strained federal government budgets, every agency is going to have to prioritize its mission and do what is done in the business world through leveraging economies of scale and scope. Having numerous federal agencies with overlapping investigative and protective responsibilities is, in my experience, not only a budget problem but a national security problem and, in the wake of the 2013 Boston terror attack, the issue should become a congressional priority.

Agencies are inherently territorial and despite post–9/11 mandates from lawmakers to better coordinate investigative missions and intelligence sharing, I have seen little progress. Protecting an agency's budget and mission will always be priority number one for managers within an agency and no congressional mandate will change that. Unless we begin to merge the rapidly multiplying federal law-enforcement workforce into a streamlined model, we will continue to see intelligence and investigative failures similar to those associated with the Boston Marathon bombing.

Unfortunately, the trend line is moving in the opposite direction as nearly a fifth of federal law-enforcement personnel are now located within smaller agencies with limited investigative authority, such as the Fish and Wildlife Service and the National Oceanic and Atmospheric Administration. How does Congress continue to justify the criminalization and subsequent investigations of American citizens for minor infractions falling under these agencies' limited purviews when we continue to miss the signs laid bare for us in the Boston terror attack investigation? We have roughly 138,000 federal law-enforcement personnel. Think of the possibilities if we reallocated agents involved in the now-infamous Fish and Wildlife Service raids on the Gibson guitar company to interviewing potential terrorists such as the Tsarnaev brothers responsible for the Boston bombing?

15

GIVING BACK THE GUN AND SHIELD

AFTER MY NEARLY FIVE YEARS of service on the PPD, it was time to move on to the next stage of my career. There are no good-bye parties when an agent departs from the PPD. You are asked to report to the administrative section to hand in your White House pass and your key to the White House grounds, and that is the extent of the "ceremony." Its banality is the very definition of the term "anticlimactic." As a courtesy from the Executive Office of the President, they offer the opportunity to join the president in the Oval Office for a series of departure photos with you and your family. I gladly took the opportunity to take the photo and was honored to be a part of it. Although my political differences with President Obama were substantial, he and his family always treated me with dignity and respect. He was one of a group of men I would have gladly sacrificed my life for. Despite the rather inglorious nature of an agent's departure from the PPD, they typically did their best to accommodate departing agents' post-PPD assignment requests, and I was grateful to be granted assignment to the Baltimore field office, located off Pratt Street in the inner harbor area of the city.

For years on the PPD I dreamt of a manageable work schedule in balance with my family life. One would think that after nearly five years of overseas travel, terrible airplane food, an entirely unpredictable schedule, exotic illnesses, and a level of fatigue that penetrates to the core, a nine-to-five position in an office would be a welcome change. Sadly, it was not.

After only a few days of settling in the Baltimore field office, I began to miss the White House's organized chaos, high-stress environment, and even the food in the White House Mess (the food service area run by the US Navy).

The Secret Service is a compartmentalized agency and when you leave one section for another, you are completely shut out of your previous division. I was the lead advance agent for the president of the United States in Afghanistan just a week prior and had left the PPD with a perfect evaluation score. I was proud of what we had accomplished during my time there. Now, I could no longer enter the White House grounds without a guest pass. It was a tough transition to handle and, although the workload in my previous position on the PPD was strenuous, it was also incredibly rewarding. I was proud of the complex security plans I successfully implemented and didn't realize how much I would miss it until I was stuck behind a desk.

I enjoyed the criminal investigative casework early in my career, but once you get a taste of protection work, there is no turning back. Having a front-row seat to the world's most important events is like an intoxicating drug. I thought back to the moment President George W. Bush spoke from the Oval Office and how I stood just feet behind the camera at the Oval Office door watching it live, and how when Bear Stearns collapsed and the gravity of the financial crisis became apparent, I was in the limo with President Bush listening to his perspective on the issue. I thought about standing in the private reading room of the Oval Office as President Bush was on the White House patio sprinting on his exercise bike at a breakneck pace and looking around at all the mementos he collected as president: a brick from the home of the spiritual head of the Taliban, Mullah Omar; the Glock pistol Saddam Hussein was carrying when he was taken into custody; and many others. This was now all part of my personal history, and they were memories that could not be forgotten and were tough to leave behind.

I knew that to keep myself from reminiscing endlessly about yesterday's accomplishments, I needed to start fresh and to find a criminal to catch. Complex criminal investigations within the federal system have a way of keeping the mind distracted and I was determined to take advantage of this. It was not long before I received a call from an agent in our Chicago field office about a fraud scheme involving apartments and rental cars. I began to investigate, and eventually uncovered what was to become one of the largest fraud schemes in Maryland's history. The case was complicated and involved a skilled con artist who manipulated low-income individuals who were down on their luck and desperately needed a car so they could get to work or a place to live. What made the case particularly egregious in my eyes was his complete lack of compassion for the victims, many of whom gave him their last dollar. When we finally arrested him in the early hours of the morning, months after the investigation began, he tried to deflect any blame and focused on the naiveté of the many victims rather than his own malice.

The case served to temporarily distract me from the nostalgia I was feeling since I left the White House, but it was only a brief respite. The local media covered the case extensively and it was featured on the front page of the *Baltimore Sun*. I was proud to have played a part in helping struggling Marylanders escape from the depravity of this con man. My first appearance on live radio was at WBAL (a radio station that later covered my campaign extensively) to discuss the case. I was nervous about the appearance because the Secret Service had a very detailed media policy and was restrictive about what could be revealed about a case and our tactics. Despite my apprehension, the appearance was enjoyable and it gave me a taste of what being in the media spotlight was all about.

With the investigative portion of the case coming to a close and the prosecution phase beginning, my job was mostly done. The fraud case was satisfying, but it was not enough to quench my desire to do something bigger. Seeing the political transformation as we moved from one administration to the next from inside the White House made the experience that much more painful for me. It seemed to me that the Obama White House staff lived in a utopian bubble devoid of any acknowledgment of real-world consequences. They spoke of policies in an idealistic way, rather than how to apply legislative solutions to the real world. When a policy not only failed to produce the desired result but in some cases produced the exact opposite result, it was ignored.

The Obamacare legislation is an obvious example. Despite the administration's stated claims about expanding health care and lowering its costs, the results have been the exact opposite. As health care costs continue to rise in excess of inflation and more and more doctors leave the field of medicine or refuse to take on any more government-sponsored cases, the administration looks on with a blind eye, seemingly proud of its good intentions yet complete lack of results. The administration persists, despite the angry town hall meetings, the poor results, and the abysmal polling, because they are insulated within the walls of the White House. The president has surrounded himself with acolytes who rarely speak truth to power. The people closest to him politically are also those he has personal relationships with, and this approach is bound to create a conflict between the real world and the artificial world of the presidency.

Having worked behind the curtain and witnessed what it is like to live "inside the bubble" of the presidency, I have seen the transformation. When you are the president of the United States, your entire life is scripted. It is almost as if you are an actor in a theatrical play about the presidency that you assumed was "real life." The president rarely drives in traffic, he never walks through airport security or waits on a tarmac, he never interacts with anyone who has not been screened by staff and law enforcement, and when he attends "public" events outside the White House, the staff screen the "public" to ensure that they fit the script. This is important because many of the bureaucrats and staffers within the Washington, DC, bubble who had a role in the design of Obamacare legislation were well aware of the media reports about the unpopularity of this legislation, and in an effort to save their careers, they relayed a completely different message to the president. Presidents are consistently surrounded by "yes men" who tell them what they want to hear, not what they need to hear.

While I was assigned to the PPD, the workload was so heavy that I rarely had time to think about my role and potential impact on the political environment. During my assignment to the Baltimore field office, I began to burn with a desire to stop watching from the front row and instead get involved in the political fight. It was at this point that I began to recall the details of my inspirational Youngstown conversation with Ken, and I began a conversation with my wife regarding a potential run for political office. We started talking seriously about the possibility of leaving the Secret Service to challenge incumbent Senator Ben Cardin in the 2012 Maryland Senate race.

Paula was adamantly opposed to a run, as was just about every other friend and family member I confided in. Respecting her wishes, I continued to drive into the Baltimore field office each day, suffering inside knowing that I could make a real difference by challenging the growing sentiment that the Democratic Party was "in it for the little guy" and Republicans were not. My own life experiences were a clear and compelling refutation of the idea that our government, although a support for some with no other options, is not the great provider of an escape route from poverty.

It took some time for my wife to warm to the idea of a campaign, but at a neighbor's party in May of 2011 she had a change of heart. The conversation turned to the path the country was on and what we were doing about it. At that moment I think she realized that running for the Senate was the perfect opportunity for me to take my political passion to the next level and use it to shake up a political process infamous for its humdrum nature. That day she affirmed her support for my decision to resign from the Secret Service and pursue Maryland's US Senate seat, and our lives would never be the same.

Although the route to work had not changed, this commute was different. I drove to the Secret Service's Baltimore field office for the last time and the decision, along with the serious consequences of failure, weighed heavily on me. I had been a Secret Service agent for twelve years. I loved my job and everything the agency stood for. The job was a lifestyle, not just a paycheck, and it was a big part of my identity. No one joins the

Secret Service to become wealthy, and it is one of the few jobs in the world whose mission is clear and simple: this president will not die today, and if he is attacked, we will die first. There is a striking nobility in that clear, simple mission. Leaving that behind for what even the most optimistic observer would call a political long shot was hands down the toughest decision I ever made.

My main concern was for my wife and daughter having to live through a campaign and a potential loss. If I stayed with the Secret Service, life would remain relatively stable. All of the trips to various countries, the coworkers I now called friends, the elation of a successfully implemented security plan, and the stress of the job's demands were all coursing through my mind. I was well aware that when I signed the paperwork declaring my intent to resign my commission as a special agent that I could not turn back. This was permanent.

The stress of the decision-making process made the short commute from my home in Severna Park to the Baltimore field office appear longer than usual. Although my wife and I were committed to the plan, I kept second-guessing and recalculating.

My phone rang during the drive and I considered ignoring it but noticed it was Paula. She had been feeling ill for a few days but we didn't think it was anything to be too concerned about. When I answered the phone she immediately said, "I'm pregnant."

The decision to resign now had ramifications for me, Paula, my daughter Isabel, and my unborn daughter Amelia. My head was in turmoil. After all, the life of a special agent is a stressful one in terms of job expectations, but not in terms of job security. I could retire in just over twelve years at the age of forty-nine with a secure pension, a lifetime guarantee of health insurance benefits, and financial stability.

"So, what do you want to do?" Paula asked me.

It seemed an unfair question. We had taken nearly five months to arrive at the decision to resign and now the circumstances were completely different. I knew if I allowed it, faith would lead me to the correct decision. I told her I would think about it over the short time remaining before I arrived at the office and would call her back.

During my twelve years in the Secret Service I met a number of exceptional people, yet one always stood above the rest. Steve, the lead advance in Trinidad, was an introspective, layered thinker and always seemed to know what was on your mind before you had the chance to tell him. When I found out that Paula was pregnant I thought of Steve's words of wisdom. He always said, "The heavens have a way of pricing things."

With that in mind, I knew the decision to take this enormous risk in resigning was the right one. I felt that if I turned back now, I would forever question what could have been. I always asked myself, "What can you live without?" My answer was that I could live without twelve more years in the Secret Service, albeit painfully, but I could not live without taking on an out-of-control government that I felt so passionately about challenging.

I drove into the field office garage, tapped the security code into the touchpad, and called Paula. "I think this is the right decision," I said.

She replied, "Me too."

With that, I parked and walked to the elevator. My supervisor, Tim, was a good man who had lost family in the 9/11 attacks on the World Trade Center. He was the first person I was going to tell, and it was going to be tough. He allowed his agents the leeway to succeed and I was determined to never let him down. I knew he would be disappointed in my decision to resign, but I hoped he would understand.

His office shared a wall with mine, and after dropping my equipment I knocked on his door. When I sat down in his office I had a hard time getting the words out. Tim was shocked, but in a refreshing break from the pessimistic responses I received from some of my friends and family, he said, "If it was anyone but you I would say this is impossible."

We talked further about the risk in leaving my job in such a terrible employment market should the campaign not succeed. My stress level was approaching critical mass when Tim made it clear to me that there would be no coming back to the Secret Service, no second chances. Running as a Republican in a blue state against an incumbent Democratic United States senator on a platform that opposed a sitting president I had protected as a Secret Service agent would effectively shut the Secret Service door forever.

I walked back to my office and sat down with the pile of administrative departure documents, and a steady stream of coworkers came into my office shocked to hear the news. Each time I told the story I began to question if it was really the right decision. Even though it has offices all over the globe, the Secret Service is a small community and as the word spread through the e-mail system like a virus, my phone began to ring. I sped up the paperwork process, unloaded my gun, and placed all of my equipment and documents in a brown paper "burn bag," a bag strictly for burning sensitive documents. I dropped it on Tim's desk, said my final good-byes, and rushed out of the office to avoid having to tell the story again. As I walked out of the field office for the last time, the sound of the thick, steel security door slamming behind me echoed through the hallway and still echoes through my mind when I think back to that day.

16

FROM BEHIND THE CAMERA TO THE FRONT

MY DECISION TO LEAVE the Secret Service and run for the United States Senate was not taken seriously by most, including many within Secret Service management. When I awoke that first Monday morning after resigning and for the first time in nearly twenty years had no assignment, I realized it was best to wait a couple of weeks before notifying the press that I was going to pursue a seat in the Senate.

On Tuesday, May 31, 2011, I was prepared to release the official announcement that I was running for the Maryland Senate seat. That morning I called one of the Secret Service deputy assistant directors and left a detailed message but received no call back. They knew that I was planning on running for the Senate but I don't believe they understood the gravity of my intentions. I was intently focused on changing the political environment in what I perceived to be a winnable race, and I was not going to be stopped. No one from the Secret Service ever bothered to call me to discuss the decision and the possible ramifications for the agency.

Before pressing the "send" button on the press release e-mail, I looked at my wife and said, "Here we go."

She appeared calm, nodded, and we let the e-mail permeate cyberspace.

I had prepared myself for releasing the decision to the press but was clearly naïve as to how much media steam the story was going to garner. Almost immediately the telephone began to ring. The shock of a Secret Service agent, largely associated with a Democratic administration, resigning to take on the Democratic Party machine in Maryland was a shock to many. I had clearly taken the local political pundits by surprise, and the requests for media appearances were seemingly endless.

My first live interview was scheduled during the afternoon drive-time radio hour with Shari Elliker of WBAL radio. Having been on a live radio program only once, discussing the fraud case with WBAL, I knew this was going to be a trial by fire. I nervously paced and quietly prayed that the appearance would be positive and allow me to build on the attention the announcement had garnered. Shari was known to give fair interviews and asked the basic questions I would hear again and again for the next two years: Why the Senate? Why not a more local office? What in your experience leads you to believe that you can perform the job of a US senator? Why resign from the Secret Service to run as a Republican in an overwhelmingly Democratic state?

I found the interview process to be easier than I expected and the stress miniscule compared to briefing the White House Situation Room via secure video link from a war zone in Afghanistan. Although thousands of people were listening, I kept reminding myself that it was just a conversation between me and Shari, and the effect was noticeable. I received warm reviews from friends and family regarding the radio show. I followed up with appearances on the conservative morning talk shows in the Maryland market. Although I was new at handling the media, I felt very comfortable and began to receive e-mails from the listeners supporting my candor and willingness to dig into economic issues. As a result of the positive media, donations started to slowly trickle into our website and the skeleton of a campaign was beginning to form.

It wasn't long after the initial burst of media attention before political opponents began to attack me on the radio and in print. A number of party "insiders" began to openly question whether I had "paid my dues" or "waited in line." I only grew more determined as they questioned my ability to take on this task in a traditionally blue state. I was focused on gaining the approval of the voters, not the party establishment, and I was determined to run my campaign on ideas and not to bow to the usual process.

The media spotlight grew in intensity as the week wore on and we struck gold just two days after the announcement when Karla, my campaign media liaison, asked me coyly if I was interested in an appearance on Neil Cavuto's show on the Fox News Channel. Any chance to appear in front of the Fox News Channel's large and loyal audience is a cherished commodity among candidates, especially conservatives. I had never done live television before. All of my prior interviews had been on the radio, and I was hoping to not only get through the interview but to get it noticed. Arriving at the New York studio and waiting in the green room was a surreal experience. I had spent twelve years surrounded by media as a Secret Service agent, but I was never the target of their attention. I had watched *Your World with Neil Cavuto* for many years and walked down the hallway to the studio confident that this was the start of something special. I sat down across from Neil, we engaged in small talk, and about ten seconds before we went live, Neil jokingly said to me, "So, are you ready for this?"

It took me slightly off guard but I quickly adjusted and after a brief introduction Neil asked, "Why are you doing this?"

My answer to the question was unrehearsed and although it lacked eloquence, I addressed the frustration I had with an unaccountable government. I said, "I just got tired of being tired. I was tired two years ago. Now I'm really tired. So I got tired of being tired and I said it's time to get in the ring and throw a few punches. It was a huge risk, no doubt about it. I gave up a great career. I love the Secret Service. They were very good to me."

He followed up midway through the interview by asking me, "Meanwhile, you want to run for senate what made you want to do it, what's lacking that you think, I have to do something?"

I spoke of my personal and political North Star, Thomas Sowell's book *The Vision of the Anointed*, and of the difference between political intentions and real-world results, and how today's Democratic Party had been wholly unable to produce tangible results. The interview was the knockout punch I needed to ensure a steady stream of media appearances and a solid introduction to the Maryland political scene. I was to appear on Neil's show multiple times throughout the campaign and will always be grateful for the chance he took on a rookie candidate.

I took the train home from New York after appearing on the weekend morning show *Fox and Friends*, where I had another solid interview. Although the media requests were still steadily streaming in to Karla, I knew I had a gargantuan task ahead of me. I had to raise a minimum of one and a half to two million dollars and build a massive team of volunteers to get the campaign moving. The media appearances helped drive traffic to my website and recruit volunteers, but I had no experience with fund-raising. I was anxious that when the media glare wore off, I would be left publicly humiliated that I couldn't get the funding I needed to run a competitive race. I was a proud man and I refused to let that happen. I decided I was going to outwork my opponents no matter what. I scheduled appearances with every political club and at any event that would have us throughout the state of Maryland, and the journey began in earnest.

17

ISRAEL AND A SURPRISE ENTRANCE INTO THE PRIMARY

DURING MY TENURE as a Secret Service agent I worked closely with the Israeli security forces, and the security of the state of Israel has always been a personal, not a political issue for me. Seeing firsthand the life-and-death security situations faced by my counterparts from Israel opened my eyes to the grave threat that they live with on a daily basis. It was hard to forget the radical Islamist taunt known by nearly every Israeli security operative: "First the Saturday people, then the Sunday people."

This speaks to an ideology that has no interest in negotiations or "peace talks"—it is interested only in death; first the death of Israel, then the death of the United States. After President Obama's infamous speech calling for the return to the 1967 borders as the basis of renewed talks, I decided that I needed to take action and show my support for Israel rather than simply speaking about it. Using my own funds, I decided to attend a rally being organized by radio host Glenn Beck in support of Israel in the summer of 2011. I was unaware at the time that the trip would change the course of my campaign and my life.

After the rally, I was scheduled to attend a dinner with Israeli and US officials along with some additional guests. There was some confusion around seating assignments and I was mistakenly placed next to Senator Mike Lee from Utah. In our subsequent conversation, I found Senator Lee to be a genuine, passionate defender of his principles rather than politics—a rare phenomenon among elected officials. I told him that I was a candidate for the US Senate in Maryland and we engaged in a nearly two-hour conversation covering everything from political philosophy to economics to constitutional law. Our discussion was refreshing, and I found it reassuring to know that there were some "good guys" left. I was privileged to be able to meet again with Senator Lee upon returning home and was thrilled when he agreed to endorse me. With little name recognition or money and involved in a race that under the best of circumstances was a long shot, I was humbled and honored by Senator Lee's support. This began a relationship that gave my campaign a credible, national profile among elected officials, which is more difficult to obtain than a credible media profile.

Despite the fortuitous set of circumstances leading to my meeting with Senator Lee, building a Republican campaign organization in a blue state from scratch was a formidable task and required a detailed strategy. The campaign schedule was filled quickly and I found myself in the car for hours each day driving from event to event. Maryland is an oddly shaped state that is too small to fly around, so all of our campaign trips were on the road. Considering my experience as an agent during three presidential campaigns, I felt that I had a good idea of the workload and the nonstop stress, but when the campaign is your own, it is very different. There are no days off on a campaign, and during the busiest days I would deliver up to ten speeches. Eating became a luxury, and I managed to locate bathrooms in every corner of Maryland. In the car shuttling between campaign stops, I spent the majority of my time on the phone trying to raise money.

Having no prior political experience, it was initially very difficult for me to raise money. There is nothing more humiliating than calling potential donors and asking for help and having them quickly reject you. But in the face of some early setbacks, I continued on and refused to give in.

I announced my candidacy in May of 2011 and for months I had the political spotlight to myself. As potential contenders for the Republican nomination began to drop out of the race, the path to the Republican primary nomination became clear. But just as the campaign seemed to hit its stride, I received an e-mail from a friend with a statement of candidacy for the 2012 Republican nomination from former deputy assistant secretary of defense Richard Douglas. His resume was impressive, and my wife and I knew immediately the political landscape had changed. The fight for the nomination would be much more challenging now, but I became more determined than ever. I didn't leave my position in the Secret Service to lose the Republican primary, and while I welcomed challengers, I was not going to lose to one.

I met Rich for the first time at the Talbot County Republican Club meeting in September of 2011 and found him to be friendly and knowledgeable. Numerous Republican Party insiders began to support Rich, and our battle for the nomination was getting more aggressive. I was never the favorite son of the Republican Party establishment, but I refused to allow this to deter me. I kept reminding myself that being an insider earned you exactly one vote, the same as the "outsiders."

18

THE CAMPAIGN
HEATS UP

AT THE MARYLAND GOP CONVENTION that fall, my campaign hosted a large hospitality area. It was the perfect opportunity to generate some additional buzz around the campaign. However, some of the attention we received was not the kind we were seeking. After a successful night interacting with supporters, I received a phone call from Brandon, a campaign staffer, telling me that his tires were flat. The following morning, I received another phone call, this time from my campaign manager, telling me that his tires were also flat. Someone placed nails in the tires of Brandon, Jim, and a third campaign staffer's cars. One week earlier we had found nails in my pregnant wife's tires, and it became clear that someone was sending us a threatening message. Sometimes the best revenge for these kinds of dirty tactics is to use them to expose your opponent. We issued a press release on the details of the incidents and publicly embarrassed the fools who did it. We never found nails in our tires again.

April 3, primary day, was an exciting one for the team. There was very little reliable polling on the race for the Republican nomination, so we could only hope for the best. Knowing the volume of work we put into the race, I was cautiously optimistic that we could pull out the victory. The night was an emotional roller coaster. As the county-by-county results came in, we would take a healthy lead, then Rich would close in, only to see us pull ahead with another county win. The results began to turn in our favor at about 10:00 that night and as our lead grew, I became more excited. Finally at 11:00 p.m., the math became insurmountable for Rich. I walked into the crowded Annapolis Marriott Waterfront ballroom and proclaimed, "We won."

It was a moment of pure elation. I never thought, considering where I started, that I would reach this point, and the excited, joyful looks on the faces of the hundreds of supporters and family members who had gathered to celebrate was a reward greater than any political victory.

I basked in the success of the primary victory for a few short days, knowing that the bigger fight was ahead of me. What I didn't know was that a media firestorm was about to hit, and a family member of mine would be at its center. Only ten days after the primary, I attended the Montgomery County GOP Lincoln dinner in one of my first official appearances as the GOP Senate nominee. While driving to the dinner I received a phone call from a former Secret Service colleague, now a high-ranking supervisor, who said, "Danno, I wanna give you a heads up. It looks like your brother's CAT [Counter-Assault Team] was caught with some locals from an okie-doke in Colombia and they're being shipped home."

His tone was humorous and intentionally cryptic and after I translated what he was telling me and asked some basic questions, it seemed that my brother, who also joined the Secret Service, was only tangentially involved and the incident was receiving little attention. Nonetheless, I was upset by the news and it weighed heavily on me the entire night. I was seated at the head table with RNC chairman Reince Priebus and was looking forward to the conversation, but was so distracted I could barely talk. The Colombia story involving Secret Service personnel and local prostitutes had not yet broken in the media, and I had no idea of the frenzy that was to come.

The story broke in the *Washington Post* later that night, and the media circus began. The campaign was flooded with requests for me, as a former Secret Service agent and now a public political figure, to comment and appear to discuss the scandal. I had yet to speak to my brother, and details on the incident were sparse even from friends still employed as special agents with the Secret Service, so I withheld comment. I desperately tried to contact active and retired agents to get information on what really happened. I needed to know the details before I could make a statement to avoid the possibility of having to make a retraction later if my facts were not accurate. As the pressure grew, I became extremely uncomfortable with our media blackout on the topic. My campaign had always been transparent and open, and I felt that our silence was lending to the appearance of impropriety, but I was having difficulty locating my brother and determining if he had played any part in this developing scandal. The facts were still unclear.

As we approached Sunday night and the attention on the story was growing, I began to reconsider our strategy of silence. Every one of our campaign consultants begged me to stay away from the scandal, but my instincts were telling me otherwise. I asked myself, "Why create suspicion?"

It came to a crescendo when a Baltimore-area radio host by the name of Sean Casey e-mailed me asking for a comment. After receiving requests from every major network, cable channel, print, and online outlet, I felt an obligation to respond to Sean. He was fair and courteous to me during the initial period of my campaign when very few people gave me a chance. I agreed to do his show that week knowing that once my voice hit the airwaves, the door for more media was wide open. I notified Karla to begin accepting interview requests and the frenzy began. Although I made no attempt to hide the fact that I had personal relationships with many of the agents involved in the scandal, I felt strongly that I should not be the one responsible for releasing their names considering the sensitive nature of the situation for the agents' families. My brother's name was supposed to be kept out of the media along with the rest of the agents involved, but someone with access to the Secret Service records of the incident leaked his name to the *Huffington Post*.

I was notified of the unauthorized leak while on the set of the MSNBC afternoon show hosted by Thomas Roberts. While waiting to go live, I noticed Karla anxiously trying to get my attention through the glass doors leading into the studio. I asked the set director to take off my microphone and he responded by saying, "You've got two minutes."

I briskly walked to the door and she said, "The *Huffington Post* has Joe's name."

I took the one minute I had left and angrily called the writer, upset at his need to publicly release my brother's name before the facts were known. I told him to do what he felt necessary, knowing that he was going to print what he wanted regardless of my feelings. I returned to the set and did the show.

Shortly after leaving the studio, I contacted my sister-in-law, who was overwhelmed and struggling to comprehend what was happening. I warned her that the media had Joe's name and was going to make it public. She was devastated. She loved my brother dearly, is a terrific mother to their two children, and was witnessing it all collapse around her.

With my sister-in-law weighing heavily on my mind, I attempted to call my brother again and this time he answered. I told him that I was furious and began to scream at him, upset at the damage this was causing our family. He told me that he had no idea what was going on, and that after he had eaten breakfast in the morning he was told to board a bus and leave Colombia. My brother explained that one of his team members had returned to the hotel with a woman and that he heard her complaining loudly in the hallway late at night. He and a Colombian police officer stationed on that floor in the hotel attempted to help her. He repeated to me again and again that he did not know what was really happening because he did not speak Spanish and she did not speak English. He insisted that he had no dealings with a prostitute.

The details of what happened in Colombia would be revealed over the course of the following days and weeks, but the personal impact on me and my family was immediate and immeasurable. My relationship with my sister-in-law and brother was damaged, my father was devastated and didn't know how to respond, and while we were dealing with the fallout in our own lives we were under an intense media spotlight. News crews were camped out in front of my brother's home twenty-four hours a day and also began knocking on my door. Both of our phones rang incessantly with interview requests and the calls began to grow increasingly hostile, with one reporter telling me, "If your brother doesn't talk I'll park a news truck outside of his front door until he changes his mind."

I did everything I could to give access to every media outlet that requested a comment. Eventually the stress of the media's intense attention began to affect my daughter. She had a difficult time comprehending what was happening and the illicit nature of the activity made it difficult for me to explain. I decided at this point to cut off all interviews on the topic and move on.

I was honest and open in my public comments on the scandal and my feelings about how it was handled and that is now a matter for history. Personally, I was furious at the White House's condescending response to the scandal and the fallout. These men erred terribly and nearly all of them paid for it by losing their jobs, some their spouses, and their reputations. The Secret Service acted quickly and immediately terminated those who broke the rules and embarrassed the agency, but ultimately, they were all men who would have given their lives for the president of the United States and his family without a second thought. Although their mistakes were now the subject of a growing international scandal, their actions never interfered with operational security and I felt the president's harsh comments were inappropriate. He failed to acknowledge that this was a pattern of behavior that was not uncommon among his own staff members within the White House and other departments in the government.

I assure you, if the same level of investigative scrutiny was applied to the White House staff members conducting advance work as was applied to the Secret Service, the results would not be flattering. In the aftermath of the scandal, the media obtained a quote from an anonymous former Secret Service agent who alluded to unscrupulous behavior at "wheels-up parties."

Wheels-up parties are informal gatherings of the entire advance team and the local officials involved in a presidential visit that occur after the president leaves town and Air Force One goes "wheels up." These largely innocuous gatherings are typically uneventful thank-yous to the local officials for their support. I always found them to be a chore, but I attended to pay my respects to the hard-working folks who make a safe visit a reality. Ironically, the only bad behavior I ever witnessed at these events was by intoxicated White House staff.

Despite the realities of both staff and agent behavior on the ground, the administration publicly berated the Secret Service and avoided any mention of cleaning up its own house. The rules seemed to apply only when there was a political advantage to be gained. Publicly attacking the Secret Service was a no-risk political play for the administration. The White House spin team knew that the Secret Service was not going to defend this abhorrent behavior and the president could appear as the disciplinarian. I blame the president's team for using the situation as an opportunity to bolster their image, knowing that it is common knowledge that some of his own people have failed to uphold this public call for higher standards of conduct. The hypocritical calls for "accountability" from the administration and certain DC lawmakers (who, allegedly, may have participated in illicit activities themselves), speaks to the untouchable attitudes of a Washington, DC, class who view American citizens as misbehaving children and themselves as the disciplinarians.

19

A POLITICAL LOSS, AND WHY ACTION MATTERS

BY THE EARLY SUMMER OF 2012, the Colombia scandal had quieted down enough for me to focus completely on the remainder of my campaign. We continued working through the summer, knocking on countless doors, making thousands of phone calls, shaking tens of thousands of hands, and attending every crab feast, barbecue, community gathering, and parade that we could fit into the schedule. Despite the great efforts of my staff, volunteers, and family, I was not optimistic on Election Day of 2012. I had no reason to be. An unexpected and unfortunate turn of events had arisen late in the campaign that made victory the longest of long shots. The campaign staff and I were completely caught off guard in late September when, with a little more than a month until the election, Rob Sobhani, a twice-failed candidate for the Republican nomination, decided to enter the race as an independent. And he had a war chest of six million dollars to finance his efforts for the remaining weeks of the campaign.

Sobhani's entrance into the race was a devastating blow to our efforts to unseat Democratic incumbent Ben Cardin, but we were not knocked completely out. We began the campaign with no infrastructure, money, media presence, or volunteers, and despite nearly insurmountable odds we managed to build a three-thousand-person-strong, statewide grassroots team. We were a fixture on local media channels and made appearances on national cable networks. We were also raising significant amounts of money, out-fund-raising both the incumbent senator and the wealthy independent combined in the closing months of the campaign. With almost two months left in the campaign, we had cut our deficit in the polls in half.

Adding to the good news was an unexpected endorsement from Senator Jim DeMint's Senate Conservatives Fund. I was honored to receive their backing and somewhat surprised at their willingness to invest in me despite the odds stacked against us. The endorsement was a testament to the organization's priority of principles over cheap politics. Yet despite all of these positive developments, the tide turned quickly when Sobhani poured much of his six-million-dollar campaign fund into a media blitz attacking my candidacy. Having to deal with the onslaught not only from Senator Cardin but now from Sobhani as well was a political Armageddon for the team and for me.

Although the campaign was realistic about our slim chances at this point, we refused to give in and continued the fight on our turf. We had the strongest grassroots effort and doubled our phone-calling and door-knocking efforts. The best we could hope for at this point was a second-place finish. I felt that if we could at least hold on to the Republican base on Election Day, it would be a testament to the power of raw determination. Our media spend was dwarfed by the competition and I had no political resume to speak of, yet we were still able to get out a clear set of ideas and principles despite the electoral fog of both the presidential election and the negative ads run by the other candidates in my race.

Election night would be emotionally difficult for me, Paula, Isabel, and the staff. While driving to the hotel ballroom near BWI Airport, which we shared with Congressman Andy Harris, it began to sink in that it was over. We were going to lose, and no amount of passion or desire to change the direction of the country could fix that.

Paula and I were quiet on the thirty-minute drive, occasionally making small talk about insignificant events to distract ourselves from the pain of losing. We both dedicated our lives and fortunes to this effort and desperately wanted to believe that it had meant something. We knew when we arrived in the work area of the hotel and joined the campaign staff that it was over. My campaign staffers were just as dedicated as my family and I were to the race, and I felt that I owed them better than this. My campaign manager, Jim Gibbons, barely left the office in the final weeks leading up to the election, and Sharon, his deputy, looked as though she had expended every ounce of energy she had within her to bring us to victory. Kelly and Ally, two of my executive staff members, were sources of strength for me and allowed me to vent my feelings during the darker moments in the campaign; they wore looks of disappointment that broke my heart. As the first counties began to report their numbers, the second-place finish became a reality.

Unfortunately, there are no silver medals in politics. Only one contender is sworn in as a United States senator, only one hand is placed on that Bible in our Capitol, and that hand was not going to be mine. My daughter Isabel was devastated. I simply could not get through to her during the campaign that our chances of winning were remote. She believed in her daddy and no one, including me, was going to convince her otherwise. I picked her up and held her tightly and shed a tear listening to her ask me repeatedly why we lost. It was tough to regain my composure, but I knew I had a job to do that night. I had to call Senator Cardin and congratulate him on his win, and then deliver a concession speech in front of the many supporters, staff, and media outlets assembled in the hotel ballroom.

My conversation with the now-reelected Senator Cardin was neither awkward nor bitter. We agreed on very little politically but never engaged in any personal attacks and had become friendly while on the campaign trail. He thanked me for running a dignified campaign and said he respected the amount of work I put in and wished me well in the future, and I responded in kind. After ending the phone call, I prepared for the last speech I was ever going to give as Maryland's 2012 Republican nominee for the US Senate.

While delivering my concession speech that night, I could see that we had done something special. I looked out at the crowd as I was speaking and did not see many dry eyes. I composed the speech in the hallway just prior to speaking and used a text message I received from a friend earlier that day as inspiration. In that message my good friend Andrew thanked me for the noble effort and asked me to read the Bible passage Timothy 4:7. I kept a miniature Bible in my car and when I opened to the verse, I read, "I have fought the good fight, I have finished the race, I have kept the faith."

I ended my speech with those words, resolved that I had done the right thing. I chose to trade financial security and a good job for the satisfaction of knowing that when it was time to take a stand and fight back, I did not stand idle.

It is easy in a country as prosperous as ours to succumb to the routine of a comfortable middle-class existence. There is a sedating quality to a life where the generational challenges of survival have largely disappeared. We live in a country and at a time where food is abundant, air-conditioned transportation awaits you in your garage, on-demand entertainment is only as far away as your remote control, and relative security in your home is the rule, not the exception. During my time and travels around the world with the Secret Service, the anesthetic of my comfortable life wore off and I became intimately familiar with the harsh realities of life outside our borders. I saw firsthand children with limbs hacked off in Rwanda who were now struggling with unimaginable health problems, Panamanian adults whose aspirations centered on basic survival rather than the American Dream of boundless prosperity, and even a French embassy employee who saw no future in his home country and told me he would do anything to become a US citizen.

When you see the contrast between our lives here in the US and the lives of citizens in nearly every other country around the world, your passion to defend the ideas that have made us exceptional can only grow. We are living in a political era where foundational American ideas—rule of law, limited government, individual liberty—have come under harsh attack, despite the undeniable prosperity, power, and success that make our country a beacon and example for the rest of the world. If you believe that today is not the best that it is ever going to be, that tomorrow can and will be better, then you need to be willing to fight for it. Fighting for it requires action, not talk. Complaining about the political course of the country may temporarily alleviate some of the frustration associated with an unwanted national decline, but it will not right the ship. If you are not satisfied, you must act. Join your local political club, help register new voters, spread the message using every platform available to you, from social media to your book club. Go to town hall meetings and refuse to be silent. Political silence is always assumed to be complacency and makes you an accomplice to those who are determined to change the fabric of this country and denigrate the principles that made it great.

But I must warn you: action changes the world, but it also attracts attention, both wanted and unwanted. There are legions of insiders who feed at the trough of the political status quo. These people are parasitic and exist in large numbers on both sides of the political fence. I witnessed this many times while working with the PPD within the walls of the White House. Access is power, and prestige and principles will always take a backseat to the desire for power. I watched scores of politicians, from the local to the national level, sell their souls in order to remain part of the "in" crowd, despite the fact that the cost of admission was selling out a former ally. Do not ever assume the loyalty of a group of politicians who you think are on your side. They will switch allegiance in a heartbeat if they think it will help them gain or retain power.

Whether you decide to become a candidate for public office or simply get involved politically as a citizen and question those who should be serving the public, be prepared for the onslaught of attacks and negative energy. I was told many times that I was a "troublemaker" and that I "kick too many barking dogs." Always remember that men and women of character are a direct threat to those politicians who are only in the game for the power. They will do anything to avoid being exposed and will confront you with all their ammunition to silence you. Principled men and women in politics often walk alone in Washington, but they attract legions of dedicated supporters in the real world of grassroots politics. Find these people and get behind them. Only after the people get involved and support the politicians who want to move this country forward—with our founding principles as a stepping-stone—will our government be returned to its rightful owner: you.

• • • • •

In recent months, several events have taken place that trouble me. The events themselves have resulted in the deaths of innocent citizens and public servants, which is disturbing in itself, but the media and the administration's handling of the issues have made the fallout even worse. Honest media coverage of these incidents would have quickly diffused any skepticism or whiff of a cover-up, and ironically, the media suppression of the stories only served to add to the scandal narrative. Some of these issues, like the Fast and Furious scandal and the Benghazi tragedy, involve the kind of complex security and military operations that I experienced throughout my career, and the mistakes are glaring. I can just imagine what is going on behind the scenes, on the secure conference calls and in the situation rooms, where administration staffers are entrenched in spinning their stories. The terrorist attack on the Boston Marathon is another example of a security failure that resulted in the loss of innocent lives. At least in the case of Boston, the administration came forward and labeled the bombing "terror" in the president's second statement about the attack. There were clearly security breaches that gave these terrorists the ability to move freely within this country and to travel back and forth to Russia without raising any red flags.

Most people probably feel like they know the facts about these important issues in our nation's modern history, but I know there is much that is unreported and the mainstream media's coverage of these issues has been inadequate at best. In the next few chapters we will spotlight these three particularly tragic examples, showing how the growing size of government bureaucracy has led to an environment of detachment, where no one is really responsible, where there is always another layer in an organization to blame for wrongdoing—and where innocent people have died as a result.

20

THE REAL SCANDAL OF "FAST AND FURIOUS"

THE HEROIC AND TRAGIC DEATH of Border Patrol Officer Brian Terry in December of 2010 was the spark that lit the powder keg of a national scandal that continues to burn. The operation, dubbed "Fast and Furious" due to the proclivity of some of the investigative targets for street racing, has been the subject of congressional inquiries, media investigations, internal US government investigations, and public scrutiny, yet the real story of what happened is still unclear.

There are a number of reasons why the truth has not come to light. The issue of firearms trafficking, unlike trafficking in narcotics or counterfeit documents (something I frequently investigated as a Secret Service agent), involves a web of political interests that even the most skilled political operative would find difficult to untangle. Despite the persistent haze surrounding the case, there are some facts that are clear. I will present what is known, but leave you with the burning question yet to be answered: were Fast and Furious weapons used on US soil, and why did the Department of Justice fail to take preventative measures?

The operation began in 2009 as a Bureau of Alcohol, Tobacco, Firearms, and Explosives (ATF) investigative effort to stem the unrelenting tide of weapons purchased illegally within the United States and trafficked across the Mexican border. I have investigated cases along with ATF agents, and I can confidently affirm that they are an elite group of men and women, dedicated to service and country. They are up against Mexican drug cartel members who use what are known in law enforcement as "straw buyers" to purchase weapons. A straw buyer is an individual who purchases a weapon on behalf of another person who, for any variety of reasons, is not eligible to purchase the weapon himself.

The case took a tragic turn and became a national story when Border Patrol Agent Brian Terry and his four-member BORTAC (Border Patrol Tactical) team came under heavy, unexpected fire after intercepting five illegal border crossers. Agent Terry was fatally wounded in the short but fierce exchange of gunfire and one of the suspects, Manuel Osario Arellanes, was taken into custody, wounded but still alive. Lying next to the body of the fatally wounded Agent Terry were weapons used by the criminals that would be traced back to the Lone Wolf Trading Company located in Glendale, Arizona. From there the national scandal began to unfold.

Internal and external politics, election cycles, Department of Justice and ATF conflicts, Second Amendment rights, and petty internal office squabbles combined in a toxic brew that became the Fast and Furious scandal. In order to explain why I place the blame largely on the Department of Justice and why I believe the death of Brian Terry may not be the last, I will have to clarify the differences between initiating, investigating, and prosecuting crimes at the federal level and at the state and local level. This important distinction is the key to the Fast and Furious case.

When I was a young police officer with the New York City Police Department, it was not uncommon to witness a street crime while on patrol, arrest the perpetrator, and give a sworn affidavit as to what you witnessed in order to establish probable cause. Probable cause is a legal requirement for any arrest regardless of the jurisdiction. In the NYPD, we witnessed a crime, arrested the suspect, and then gathered the investigative details.

Establishing probable cause and making an arrest in the federal system usually works in the opposite direction. Federal agents will typically investigate the case thoroughly first, establishing probable cause in the process, then make a phone call to an "intake" assistant United States attorney (AUSA) to determine if he will agree to accept the case for potential prosecution. If the AUSA agrees to prosecute the case in the federal system, arrest warrants will be issued and the suspects will be taken into custody, but not until an overwhelming amount of evidence has already been collected. Very few AUSAs want to take cases that may go to trial, so the bar for acceptance by the attorney is high. Usually the AUSA wants to see enough evidence to force a plea bargain so a trial will not even be considered an option. The politics of justice at the federal level dictate that numbers matter, because numbers can be used by politicians and bureaucrats to further their careers. Falling crime rates are electoral gold and so are successful federal prosecutions. This gives US attorneys much incentive to make sure that they don't take on a case that they have even the slimmest chance of losing.

Why does the process matter? Because what is known in federal law-enforcement jargon as a "PC arrest" (short for probable cause arrest) is a rare and strongly discouraged enforcement tool in the federal system. Police officers at the state and local level use their probable cause arrest authority every day to keep our neighborhoods safe. Yet federal agents, many of whom are former police officers, are strongly discouraged from making this type of arrest. They must follow the established federal procedure of completing an investigation and getting AUSA approval before moving forward with an arrest. If it appears counterintuitive that well-trained, well-educated federal agents cannot do what our police officers on the street do every day, that's because it is. By nature, a probable cause arrest is unpredictable, and unpredictability is the enemy of our federal justice system. Everyone from the magistrate judges, to the intake AUSA, to the assigned AUSA, to the US Marshal's Service, which will handle the prisoner, are all on relatively consistent work schedules. The fastest way to get on the bad side of the United States Attorney's Office is to start making PC arrests late at night without having thoroughly exhausted all investigative avenues, completed mounds of paperwork, and made an appointment with the AUSA for an arrest. Yes, an appointment.

Unless the case is a justifiable emergency, a PC arrest is a virtual career death sentence. It is likely that none of your future cases will be accepted for prosecution if you get on the bad side of an AUSA. In this system the AUSA has broad latitude, and the PC arrest scenario is just one example of the power they hold. Based on my experience, I am confident that this power structure played a pivotal role in the tragic Fast and Furious operation.

The generally held belief around the operation, which has been supported by the media, is that ATF agents let guns "walk," i.e., be purchased illegally and not tracked, and this misstep led to the tragic death of Brian Terry. After reading and analyzing multiple accounts of the circumstances surrounding the investigation, I do not believe this to be the case. From all accounts, the seven ATF agents of Group VII, led by case agent Hope MacAllister, were dedicated, nonideological federal operators genuinely trying to stop illegal gunrunning into Mexico. Allowing guns to "walk" is not a sanctioned investigative tactic, and I do not believe this was Group VII's intention.

The trafficking of firearms from straw buyers is a federal crime, but if there is no one willing to prosecute the case, then it has the same effect of a tree falling in the woods—no one can hear it. Katherine Eban of *Forbes* magazine states in her June 27, 2012, piece that, "By January 2010 the agents had identified 20 suspects who had paid some $350,000 in cash for more than 650 guns. According to Rep. Issa's congressional committee, Group VII had enough evidence to make arrests and close the case then."

In my experience investigating similar cases at the federal level involving the purchasing of contraband, Assistant United States Attorney Emory Hurley, working with MacAllister and the agents of Group VII, could have easily moved forward with prosecution. The evidence in the case was overwhelming. It included the repeated cash purchases of expensive firearms by purchasers with no financial ability to support this type of activity. In the summer of 2010, a straw buyer cooperating with Group VII agent John Dodson delivered weapons to a suspected gun trafficker and provided wiretap recordings of the illicit transactions, and still no arrests were made. Former ATF attaché in Mexico Darren Gil may have stated it best when, in response to questions on the progress of the investigation, he said, "Again, spring time it got to the point of . . . at what point are we going to close this investigation down? I mean, after 500 or so seizures I think you should have enough data collection on what you're trying to show or prove. It was my position, it was Chief [Dan Kumor's] position as well. He says, yeah, you're right. And he goes, 'So when are they going to close this down?' And we were both on the same position there that this thing needed to be shut down."

Never in my experience as a federal agent have I heard of an investigation with this much evidence and no indictments or arrest warrants. Receiving judicial approval for a federal wiretap alone takes an enormous amount of evidence. Every practical tool in the investigative toolbox must be exhausted before a federal judge will approve a wiretap. The fact that Group VII acquired wiretap authority indicates to me that the case had proceeded far past the stage of just reasonable suspicion and was known to DOJ headquarters. Any efforts by DOJ headquarters to claim ignorance of the case details prior to the tragic death of Agent Terry are suspicious at best. In the spring of 2010 the application for the federal wiretap was signed on behalf of Assistant Attorney General Lanny Breuer through DOJ's Office of Enforcement Operations.

In a perfect world, the agents of Group VII would have ended the stream of weapons crossing the border and made probable cause arrests like any local police officer. But, it is not a perfect world, and in federal law enforcement an ever-growing army of agents insulated within competing agencies and rarely interacting with each other are forced to compete for the limited time of the US Attorney's Office, and you cannot afford to find yourself on the receiving end of their wrath or you will be ignored. Combine this dynamic with the bureaucratic DOJ and its constantly expanding layers of hierarchy designed to insulate those at the top from having to take any responsibility for what is actually happening on their watch and you have the ingredients for a tragedy.

Solidifying my suspicions that probable cause was abundant and arrests should have taken place is the fact that within twenty-four hours of the death of Border Patrol Agent Brian Terry, an arrest was made.

Jaime Avila, suspected of purchasing two of the weapons found alongside the body of Agent Terry, was arrested, and nineteen additional suspects were indicted two weeks later on January 19, 2011. Does this make sense to you? Seven veteran ATF agents investigate a gun trafficking ring for nearly a year, using every tool available to modern law enforcement, and they cannot develop a legally sound case? But magically, within twenty-four hours of Agent Terry's murder, DOJ and the Arizona US Attorney's Office decide the case is worth prosecuting. This reeks of prosecutorial laziness, ineptitude, and arrogance.

I am confident that the US Attorney's Office was anxious about potentially losing the case if it went to trial, despite the reams of evidence, and chose to let the case fester. The insensitive DOJ bureaucracy and the diffused responsibility incentivized the US attorneys to produce strong prosecution numbers that can be marketed politically, rather than pursue cases that have more value to the public. They were moved to action only when they realized that there would be severe political ramifications after the highly publicized death of Agent Terry and from the investigation that would follow. Their laziness and lack of integrity had real-world consequences, and despite the numerous warnings from the ATF agents on the ground who were sounding the alarms, the DOJ acted only when there was a political cost to pay.

The ATF agents of Group VII were forced into a losing proposition by the US Attorney's Office. They could not arrest the suspects, even though they had more than enough evidence, because probable cause arrests were frowned upon by the AUSA. But they could not abandon the case and allow the weapons trafficking to continue unabated. Regardless of the ATF's actions, guns were going to "walk" across the border, and prosecutorial and bureaucratic ineptitude would be to blame. No federal agent ever wants to be in this kind of scenario, where bloodshed is the result of a crime you know you could have prevented.

In addition, Department of Justice headquarters cannot claim that they were unaware of the potential danger of inaction, because AUSA Joe Cooley was briefed personally on the significance of the case on March 5, 2010. Cooley attended the meeting at ATF headquarters on behalf of Assistant Attorney General Lanny Breuer and was briefed by Group VII supervisor David Voth on the troubling specifics of the case. According to

ATF officials, the attendance of a DOJ headquarters representative at these briefings was unusual. In addition, according to the Joint Staff Report produced for Congress, the special agent in charge of the ATF's Dallas office, Robert Champion, expressed anxiety about the growing number of weapons sourced to Fast and Furious. During a video conference he asked, "What are we doing about this?"

DOJ headquarters, represented at the meeting by AUSA Cooley, stated in response that the volume of the illegal trafficking was "an acceptable practice." It was not.

A media frenzy ensued when it was uncovered that Fast and Furious weapons were used in the slayings of Mexican citizens; however few in the media bothered to ask if Fast and Furious guns were used on US soil. It continues to baffle me why this question has eluded many investigative journalists. With over a hundred high-powered weapons recovered from crime scenes in Mexico, based on my analysis of the data in this case, that must be the tip of the iceberg.

Here are some of the data that I believe show that Fast and Furious weapons have been used on United States soil, and that the DOJ bureaucracy knew about it and did nothing to stop it:

> On January 13, 2010, agents in the ATF's Dallas office seized forty weapons in El Paso, Texas, that were traced back to a straw purchaser who was the subject of Group VII's Fast and Furious investigation. ATF agents suspect that these weapons were being used by Mexican cartel operatives to help gain control of a prolific drug trafficking corridor.

> An analysis of publicly available trace data from the ATF points to a suspicious pattern of weapon recoveries at crime scenes. Prior to the initiation of the Fast and Furious investigation in 2009, it was relatively uncommon to recover a weapon from a crime scene in New York that had originally been purchased in Arizona. Yet in 2010, after the case began, Arizona rose into the top fifteen sources for weapons recovered at New York crime scenes and remained so through 2011.

> The number of firearms recovered from crime scenes in Texas, and sourced to Arizona, numbered 56 in 2009, making it the eleventh largest source of recoveries by state. Yet in 2010, Arizona-sourced recoveries more than doubled to 128, moving Arizona up to the third largest source state for recoveries.

Firearms recovered from crime scenes in California, and sourced to Arizona, numbered between 832 and 846 from 2008 to 2010, yet jumped to 995 in 2011.

According to a Joint Staff Report produced for Congress and released on July 26, 2011, ATF Group VII supervisor David Voth sent an e-mail to William Newell, who was then special agent in charge of the Phoenix office, at 7:22 p.m. on Thursday, December 16, 2010, incredibly stating that 350 weapons were recovered within the United States that could be sourced to the Fast and Furious investigation.*

When looking at these data, it is not difficult to conclude that these weapons were not only found but used on American soil, despite the lack of media coverage on the topic. Federal restrictions prevent trace-data specifics, such as the federal firearm licensee who sold the firearm, from being publicly released, but it is my unfortunate conclusion that the connection eventually will be made. One of these weapons is going to be tied to a crime on United States soil. It is only a matter of time. This dangerous consequence of the Department of Justice's failure to vigorously and promptly act on the illegal trafficking of high-powered firearms has shocked some, but sadly it does not surprise me.

---

* Information on the El Paso seizure was taken from a US Congress Joint Staff Report issued on July 26, 2011, entitled *The Department of Justice's Operation Fast and Furious: Fueling Cartel Violence*, http://narcosphere.narconews.com/userfiles/70/Sinaloa.ATF-07-26-11-Report-on-Impact-on-Mexico-2.pdf. Information on trace data from the ATF was referenced from http://www.atf.gov/statistics/trace-data/index.html.

21

BENGHAZI: WHO GAVE THE ORDER TO STAND DOWN?

DURING MY TWELVE-YEAR CAREER as a special agent with the United States Secret Service, I was honored to serve with some of the finest military and law-enforcement personnel in the world. I was consistently humbled by the character of the men and women in our military who, for little money and even less fame, agree to protect this nation with their lives so millions of Americans can sleep peacefully at night. The battle-hardened special operators who served as a counterassault team in Indonesia and were willing to perform any task in service to our mission of keeping the president safe, and the Delta Force operator in Afghanistan whose blank stare clearly captured the emotional suppression of all he had seen and done in service to our country, served as inspiring portraits of courage and sacrifice for me.

Although being a Secret Service agent is an extremely stressful position, I never felt underappreciated or undercompensated, and I always regretted the fact that my words of thanks to the members of our military whose paths I would intersect never really captured the true depth of my appreciation. These men and women work long hours under the harshest of conditions and in the most dangerous environments in the world, and all for little pay. My brief and sometimes incomplete words of appreciation were a small token of gratitude to a group of men and women who deserve far more.

When I initially heard on the news about the tragic events in Benghazi, Libya, on September 11, 2012, I assumed it was a mistake or poor reporting. Having been assigned to many protective details for foreign leaders, dignitaries, and of course the president, I had a long history of working with the Diplomatic Security Service, the security and protection branch of the US Department of State. The reports that the ambassador to Libya, Christopher Stevens, was unaccounted for were unbelievable to me. I could not imagine a scenario in which an ambassador would be missing and possibly dead under their watch.

The Diplomatic Security Service is an elite group of men and women who surely had a fully equipped and fully manned security team on the scene, given that they were conducting operations in an active conflict zone. I was also shocked by reports of the alleged communication breakdown during the assault on our diplomatic mission in Benghazi. From my years in the White House constantly shadowing the president, I saw how he and his top officials had instantaneous access to information. When anything significant occurs, the president or a pertinent cabinet member is made aware of it by multiple means of communication. They receive e-mail, phone briefings, personal briefings, and a near-endless supply of briefing documents, which are constantly updated. The alleged lack of information filtering up to the president and secretary of state regarding the unfolding emergency in Libya was in direct conflict with my personal experience within the walls of the eighteen-acre White House complex.

Analyzing Benghazi as someone who has experienced the behind-the-scenes workings of the White House and made a career of managing risk and mitigation, there are three specific areas of concern that I found especially alarming, and they all relate to the DC web of bureaucracy getting in the way of operations on the ground. First, the inadequacy of the security detail was not at all commensurate with the threat level in an active conflict zone. Second, the information stream disseminated by the White House and other administration surrogates was not consistent with any prior crisis-management message strategy I ever witnessed in two presidential administrations, and it directly conflicted with the accounts of personnel on the ground and even with information coming from within the government. Third, the survivors of the Benghazi attack seemingly disappeared and were not made readily available to either the media or our elected representatives for questioning.

My first concern centers on the assigned protection team and the security plan in place on the night of the attack. When a United States government official is assigned a protective detail from the growing army of siloed and distinct federal agencies that provide this service, manpower and equipment are allocated according to a threat assessment based on intelligence reports. This assessment is a thorough analysis of the current and potential threats that could endanger the protectee and any support personnel. It takes into account the protectee's diplomatic status, the geographic environment he operates in, and his potential value to our enemies as the target of an attack. Using this methodology, the agents who design the protection plan can determine the number of agents to assign to the protective detail; the weaponry they carry; the number of vehicles required and the armor capabilities of those vehicles; the number, if any, of special weapons teams to assign; the use of military assets, to include special ops forces if necessary; the level of security necessary at the physical sites where the protectee will live, work, and visit; and a multitude of other details that encompass the art of building a well-designed security plan.

I worked often with the superb agents of the Diplomatic Security Service and was immediately surprised to learn from a friend that there was no Mobile Security Deployment (MSD) tactical team assigned to Ambassador Stevens while he was in Benghazi on the night of September 11, 2012. This cadre of highly trained special weapons operators normally serves on high-risk protection details and carries advanced weapons designed to thwart and counter any potential attack against a high-value target. Why were these men, the best-trained and most highly skilled protection agents the DSS has in its arsenal, not being used when a United States ambassador was present in an active conflict area? As many as twenty-one members of this skilled unit were in Libya less than a year earlier with former ambassador Gene Cretz. Why were they removed?

It is clear that officials within the DSS knew the security footprint assigned to Ambassador Stevens was insufficient, and despite their warnings and requests, the deficient protection plan tragically persisted. Ambassador Stevens was aware of the inadequate security and expressed concerns with the loss of the MSD teams when he wrote in a May 2012 e-mail to State Department official John Moretti that he and his team "would feel much safer if we could keep two MSD teams with us through this period." The request was denied.

Eric Nordstrom, the DSS regional security officer with supervisory oversight over the detail assigned to Ambassador Stevens, testified to lawmakers following the Benghazi attack that he requested five DSS agents be stationed at the mission. The response he received from Deputy Assistant Secretary Charlene Lamb was that "[she] believed the Benghazi post did not need any Diplomatic Security special agents because there was a residential safe haven to fall back to in an emergency, but that she thought the best course of action was to assign three agents."

Three DSS agents in an active conflict zone, with no MSD tactical support, dictated by a bureaucrat with no security experience is a stunning act of either incompetence or malfeasance. Unfortunately, it is completely consistent with what I saw from insulated career bureaucrats who overestimated their own skills at the expense of the analysis of trained professionals.

What makes Lamb's denial of the security request even more perplexing is that, based on my experience, the request for even five DSS agents (the actual number present on the night of the attack due to temporarily assigned duty personnel being present in country) was grossly insufficient and was probably driven by a frustration with the bureaucratic process. It means that the DSS and/or the ambassador were willing to accept an increased security threat because they knew it wasn't worth trying to fight the State Department for adequate assets.

Mr. Nordstrom further testified before the House Oversight and

Government Reform Committee that Lamb "wanted to keep the number of US security personnel in Benghazi artificially low." He also commented to the regional director of the agency's Bureau of Near Eastern Affairs that "for me, the Taliban is on the inside of the building."

Nordstrom's statements are disturbing because they point to political decision making rather than decision making based on proven protection methodologies and experience-driven threat assessments from a security professional. I share his frustration.

The inadequate security footprint did not go unnoticed by military officials in the region looking to assist. Lieutenant Colonel Andrew Wood noted the discrepancy between the security the bureaucrats at the State Department were considering and what was actually required after a number of foreign governments and NGOs withdrew from the area. According to a congressional report, he testified, "It was apparent to me that we were the last flag flying in Benghazi. We were the last thing on their target list to remove from Benghazi."

To provide some perspective, when I planned President Obama's security operation in Afghanistan, there were thousands of people integrated into the security plan from both federal law enforcement and the US military. This operation was conducted on a secure US military base, and even with the incredible level of participation from all of those mentioned, I still had very serious security concerns.

Now, compare this to the security footprint surrounding Ambassador Stevens on the night of the attack. He had only five DSS agents with no Mobile Security Deployment tactical team and no assigned military special forces support. Does this appear logical to you? It does not require advanced US Secret Service training to determine that the bureaucrats who inserted themselves into the security decision-making chain were motivated by politics, not a legitimate concern for security. They cared more about advancing the president's narrative that "al-Qaeda is on the run" than protecting our diplomats and military who serve this country. If only Ambassador Stevens, Sean Smith, Glen Doherty, and Ty Woods could have known earlier that their lives were the payoff in a series of bad bets that bureaucrats made to preserve their political futures, maybe they would be alive today.

Of course, politics getting in the way of security is nothing new. I was involved in a number of security operations where staff at the senior level of the White House and other departments attempted to manipulate the security plan for political reasons, but I never allowed it to impact our operation. I always felt that the PPD managers would defend my decisions, and whenever there was a conflict between staff and Secret Service, we had to "kick it up the chain" to a senior member of the agency who would support us. Once a conflict was elevated to PPD management, security frequently won out over politics. So why was Eric Nordstrom ignored?

I suspect it was for political reasons, not only within the State Department but larger electoral politics as well. The president's reelection campaign was in full swing at the time of the attack, and political victories supersede nearly everything for a staff member. If Lamb and others within the State Department acknowledged, less than two months before the election, that the situation in Libya had deteriorated significantly, there would be a severe price to pay. It would be proof that the president's signature foreign policy initiatives in the Middle East were on the verge of collapse. It would show that terrorists were still a very real threat to Americans, and that wouldn't get President Obama more votes. Future promotion or a prestigious new assignment would be in jeopardy for any staff member who was part of the decision to formally acknowledge a deteriorating security situation.

But what Lamb and her cadre of State Department bureaucrats failed to take into account was that by assigning DSS protection to Ambassador Stevens, they would be forced to deal with agents and supervisors who refused to play politics. The nonpolitical nature of Nordstrom's position enabled him to honestly assess the situation and request support commensurate with the threat level. The situation became muddled only when those with political rather than security interests became intertwined in the decision chain. Lamb and others likely assumed that nothing would happen to our personnel in Benghazi, and even when offered military resources at no cost to the State Department, her staff responded that Lamb was reluctant to accept this support because it would be "embarrassing to continue to have to rely on DOD [Department of Defense] assets to protect our mission."

Her apparent concern with political embarrassment rather than the safety of American personnel is indicative of the pervasive feeling among our bureaucratic elite that they can hide among the diffuse responsibility of their enormous organizations. After all, in a bureaucracy as large and notorious as that of the State Department, surely there would be an underling to blame or a memo they could claim they failed to see in the unlikely event that something tragic were to happen. Secretary of State Hillary Clinton, an outspoken advocate for expansive government, failed to see the hypocrisy of her own ideology when she testified before the House Foreign Affairs Committee that cables addressed specifically to her requesting an increased security footprint in Benghazi did not in fact come to her. Clinton said, "They [the cables] do not all come to me. They are reported through the bureaucracy."

What saddens me most is that the bureaucratic class likely views this tragedy as "the price of doing business," and the security teams, despite their willingness to serve in Benghazi, were just following orders, despite what I consider a criminally inadequate security plan.

Not only was the security decision-making process prior to the attack politicized, but decisions made while the attack was underway were also severely lacking and did not follow what I remember to be procedure for such a serious event.

In the aftermath of the 1979 Iranian hostage crisis and the subsequent analysis of how to prevent events like that from occurring again, the military refined a global response plan for attacks on American embassies overseas. As such, we had military forces willing and able to launch a rescue attempt of our personnel during the Benghazi attack, but a number of still hazy factors prevented them from receiving orders to deploy until nearly five hours after the initial assault began. After a military unit relocated from a training mission in Croatia to Southern Europe and was activated to provide assistance to the Benghazi mission, nothing happened. This is where their story ends.

We must ask the question: who gave the order to stand down, and why?

More disturbing is the lack of action by a multiagency unit known as FEST. FEST stands for Foreign Emergency Support Team and it consists of highly trained personnel from a number of federal agencies who are specifically tasked with providing timely support to US personnel in crisis overseas. That this team was not activated is beyond suspicious, because their mandate is to respond to *exactly* the sort of emergency that occurred in Benghazi. It is the equivalent of the Secret Service being told to stand down during an attack on the president.

Another striking example of how the Benghazi attack was mishandled is the clearly misleading information stream emanating from the administration after the attack. Based on my experiences embedded in two presidential administrations, there are controls in place to ensure information is disseminated only after being vigorously vetted through specific individuals who are responsible for the administration's communications. I have never been involved in any presidential visit, domestic or foreign, where message control was not the highest priority. Yet the stream of information relayed by the president and the State Department after the Benghazi attack was obviously false and clearly politically motivated.

The timing of the Benghazi attack being so close to the presidential election likely set off a flurry of activity and panic in and around the White House. The White House hums with activity when it is conducting the normal business of governing, and when that hum is interrupted, everything changes. Staffers begin to move from their standard pace to a hurried walk, facial expressions of concern are obvious, motorcades begin to line up on West Executive Avenue, and high-ranking government officials usually not seen at the White House begin to show up in the cramped hallways of the West Wing.

When the attack occurred at 9:40 p.m. local time in Benghazi, it was 3:40 in the afternoon at the White House. This is the very heart of the presidential workday, and it is highly unlikely that the first piece of information the president received was about a group of protesters angry over the now-infamous Internet video disrespecting Muhammad. This is important, because although we now know the protest story to be untrue, if there is not a shred of evidence that a protest was even mentioned by any of the personnel on the ground and who were actively communicating with Washington, then one must ask why the administration completely fabricated such a story. Lying about the events that night is a disgrace to the memories of the men who sacrificed their lives during that attack. I witnessed crisis management in action at the White House, and there are priorities for each administration and a plan for handling breaking news. Clearly the priority for this administration was political spin first, and safety and security second. The facts about the incident laid bare by the State Department's Accountability Review Board make it clear that there was a deliberate attempt to cover up the truth of what occurred at the diplomatic mission in Benghazi on September 11, 2012.

The ARB report describes how within minutes of the attack, an agent from the Diplomatic Security Service (identified in the report as ARSO 1), in the process of evacuating and securing Ambassador Stevens, gave Stevens his cell phone. At that point Stevens began making calls for assistance. The report states that Stevens called "local contacts" and the embassy in Tripoli for assistance. Also, the report makes mention of a 9:50 p.m. local time call between Stevens and the deputy chief of mission, Gregory Hicks, regarding the attack. According to Hicks's account, which he relayed to Utah Representative Jason Chaffetz during congressional hearings, Ambassador Stevens shouted to Hicks through the cell phone, "We're under attack. We're under attack." Hicks also recounted how he "immediately called into Washington to trigger all the mechanisms."

The embassy in Tripoli, notified of the attack at approximately 9:45 p.m. local time, set up a command center and contacted Washington. Pursuant to the embassy's notification of the attack, Department of Defense personnel relocated an unarmed surveillance drone that arrived at 11:10 p.m. local time, "shortly before the DS [Diplomatic Security] team departed."

According to the report, there was no mention of a protest in the communication with Tripoli, only an attack. In addition, in an "Ops Alert" issued shortly after the attack began, the State Department Operations Center notified senior department officials, the White House Situation Room, and others that the Benghazi compound was under attack and that "approximately twenty armed people fired shots; explosions have been heard as well." Two hours later, the Operations Center issued an alert that al-Qaeda linked Ansar al-Sharia (AAS) claimed responsibility for the attack and had called for a second assault on the embassy in Tripoli. Neither alert mentioned that there had been a protest at the location of the attacks.

Several hours later the report notes that, "In Washington, at 10:32 p.m., an officer in the National Military Command Center at the Pentagon, after receiving initial reports of the incident from the State Department, notified the Office of the Secretary of Defense and the Joint Staff.

The information was quickly passed to Secretary of Defense, Mr. Leon E. Panetta, and the Chairman of the Joint Chiefs of Staff, General Martin E. Dempsey. Secretary Panetta and General Dempsey attended a previously scheduled meeting with the president at the White House at 11:00 p.m., approximately eighty minutes after the attack began. The Defense Department reported that principals discussed potential responses to the ongoing situation."

Our involvement in the Libyan conflict in the months prior to the Benghazi attack provided an extensive intelligence, military, and DSS footprint in the region and on the ground, especially in the aftermath of the death of Libyan dictator Muammar Gaddafi. It is highly improbable that all of these trained, dedicated individuals relayed inaccurate information to their Washington, DC, chain of command. Furthermore, with the ubiquitous presence of smartphones, Internet-based radio transmissions, satellite phones, e-mail, classified computer networks, and airborne surveillance technology, it is nearly impossible to have a complete communication breakdown with senior officials in Washington. It is clear from reports on the incident that communication was immediate and ongoing, and status updates originating from both the ground in Benghazi and the embassy in Tripoli were frequent—and none made mention of any protest. It borders on the absurd to believe that the administration and its surrogates actually thought that the Benghazi attack was due to a protest about an anti-Muslim Internet video.

All of this evidence, however, did not stop the administration from shifting into damage-control mode. Just one day after the attack the White House made a statement: "Since our founding, the United States has been a nation that respects all faiths. We reject all efforts to denigrate the religious beliefs of others."

Notice the careful use of the language in the administration's attempt to craft a theme about the attack. The choice of words intentionally diverts any blame from the president's foreign policy choices and focuses instead on religious persecution. They were also careful to avoid saying that the offensive video caused the attack, but they were clearly laying the groundwork for a theme by simply correlating the attack with religion, even though they had absolutely no evidence that the video and the attack were related. They were testing the message here without committing to it, which is a common tactic in political circles. "Trial balloon" messaging is a standard practice where a message is floated and the staff watches closely to see how the public and media respond.

Initially, when it seemed that the press was buying into the Internet video explanation, the White House hallways were likely buzzing with glee. More infuriating is the fact that their arrogance regarding the lies they were spewing even led them to spend taxpayer dollars to promote the administration's story. Our government spent $70,000 on an advertising initiative in Pakistan directly after the attack in order to distance the United States from the Internet video they knew had nothing to do with the events in Benghazi.

As the days in early September passed, the administration continued to move its message forward. On September 14, Secretary of State Clinton stated, "We've seen the heavy assault on our post in Benghazi that took the lives of those brave men. We've seen rage and violence directed at American embassies over an awful Internet video that we had nothing to do with." Again, the mention of the video in connection with the attack further solidifies the message, and again the administration waited for the serious media inquiries to begin. It did not happen.

The administration's bogus account of the cause of the Benghazi attack hit a crescendo on September 16 when US ambassador to the United Nations Susan Rice went on all the Sunday morning political talk shows promoting this message. She made the now-infamous comments, "There was a hateful video that was disseminated on the Internet. It had nothing to do with the United States government and it's one that we find disgusting and reprehensible. It's been offensive to many, many people around the world. That sparked violence in various parts of the world, including violence directed at Western facilities including our embassies and consulates. That violence is unacceptable. It's not a response that one can ever condone when it comes to such a video. And we have been working very closely and, indeed, effectively with the governments in the region and around the world to secure our personnel, secure our embassy, and condemn the violent response to this video."

Ambassador Rice's statements demonstrate the arrogance in the administration's deceit. Her appearances on the closely watched Sunday talk show circuit shows the full commitment to the Internet video story at this point. The levels of government bureaucracy involved in vetting the talking points for a high-level official going on the Sunday political talk show circuit are numerous, thorough, and designed to insulate decision makers from blame when bad decisions are made. In a perfect world, if Susan Rice made a mistake, then surely someone would be eager to correct it, but that is not how the bureaucracy is designed to function. Principled public servants are silenced and threatened if they attempt to deviate from the political agenda. The "I was just following orders" mentality and diffuse responsibilities ensured that no one person had to shoulder the guilt of the tangled web of lies and deceit the administration spun.

If the politicization of the lives of our patriotic public servants and the intentionally misleading information disseminated by the administration are not enough to convince you that something suspicious is going on, ask yourself this: why were the survivors of the Benghazi attacks hidden?

No one disputes that there were several Americans serving in Benghazi on the night of the fateful attack, but as for their numbers or their location, details were intentionally hidden. Information leaks in Washington are so numerous that during my time with the Secret Service, they were typically factored into our plans. It was assumed that information would leak, and layered security plans designed to handle leaks were the rule, not the exception. Yet after the Benghazi attacks on both the diplomatic mission and the CIA annex, the survivors received medical attention in Benghazi, were moved to an airfield, transported first to Tripoli and then back to the United States, and treated at a facility at home, all the while hidden from the press and public.

That all of this action was taken without *any* information leaking to the media is an act of logistical secrecy I have never witnessed during all my time with the government. Given all of the people involved in all aspects of the incident, it is amazing that no information about the survivors was leaked. Keeping a secret in the federal government is exceedingly difficult, because trafficking in information, both classified and unclassified, is big business in Washington. During both my run for the US Senate and my tenure as an agent, I was appalled by the sheer number of individuals eager to scoop a story. Everyone wants to be in the "information in-crowd," and the appetite for inside information from journalists, bloggers, and corrupt bureaucrats looking for some detail to use as political ransom is insatiable.

The question is not *if* information is going to leak, but *when*.

Yet even in this environment, time passed and a thick blanket of secrecy remained over the location and condition of the Benghazi survivors. I was in awe of the intricate level of detail involved with keeping the Benghazi survivors' location a secret and the preventative mechanisms put in place to silence anyone who had knowledge of the situation from speaking out. Even now, almost a year after the incident, CNN has reported on an unprecedented internal effort to ensure the silence of CIA personnel with knowledge of the Benghazi affair.**

In a March 1, 2013, letter to Secretary of State John Kerry, Representatives Frank Wolf and Jim Gerlach cite a "reliable source" who indicated that there were as many as thirty survivors of the attack and that many of them were being treated at Walter Reed National Military Medical Center. If this was this case, the effort to silence the survivors was even more unprecedented. Something has been exchanged for their cooperation, and it must be significant. It was only after relentless congressional, public, and media pressure that Gregory Hicks, deputy chief of mission in Tripoli, and Mark Thompson, deputy coordinator for operations for the State Department's counterterrorism bureau, were located and authorized to testify before Congress about the numerous failures leading to the deaths of our personnel in Benghazi and the sad cover-up that followed.

But the political penalty to be paid by those working overtime to suppress the Benghazi survivors' accounts of the incident is likely going to be severe. Every political consultant can attest to the fact that an issue becomes much more personal when you can put a human face on it. The Benghazi survivors eventually will recount, in tragic detail, the events of September 11, 2012; the fear, shock, and disappointment they felt at the utter lack of any significant US military or diplomatic response to an attack that lasted more than eight hours; and the anger at becoming pawns in the administration's cover-up.

Tears tell a story words can never adequately replicate, and the officials involved in the deliberate suppression of information are well aware of this fact. A word of caution to the administration: as time passes, secrets become less secret, threats become less threatening, and promises become less rewarding. This information will leak out over time; indeed it has

---

** http://thelead.blogs.cnn.com/2013/08/01/exclusive-dozens-of-cia-operatives-on-the-ground
-during-benghazi-attack/?on.cnn=1.

begun to come out already. Every detail of the survivors' accounts of the attack will reopen a gaping wound and destroy any semblance of credibility this administration may have left. The bureaucracy is an imperfect shield, and it can save the administration and its surrogates only for a limited amount of time.

22

BOSTON: TOO MANY AGENCIES, NOT ENOUGH COMMUNICATION

THE APRIL 15, 2013, terrorist attacks in Boston opened up a new chapter in our ongoing battle against terrorism. In a country where we attribute our success and prosperity to both economic and political liberty, which we extend to everyone within our borders, it is a tragedy that those who have enjoyed these freedoms still make America their target of choice. Terrorists who continue to target us subscribe to an ideology that is the very antithesis of freedom. Their ideology is one anchored in blame and pursues a goal of global hegemony and forced sub-servience. They use the tools of terror, death, and destruction to achieve these perverse goals. This is not about religion. There are three million Muslims currently living peacefully in the United States who would be revolting en masse if this were a religious issue. Rather, it is about a group of murderers attempting to hijack and hide behind religion in order to lend some air of legitimacy to their evil ambitions.

The Obama administration's obvious discomfort with publicly acknowledging terrorism is a by-product of the president's ideological belief system, which tends to the extreme left. The extreme left wing of the Democratic Party is led by politicians who believe that society can be perfected, that evil is simply a by-product of a societal breakdown, and that the historical mistakes of the United States are the cause of our current global challenges. It is this type of idiocy that is exposing the American people to unnecessary dangers as Washington avoids the warning signs of international and domestic terrorism in a misguided effort to not cast blame.

Having spent many years behind the curtain as a federal agent, I can attest to the damage a dangerously ignorant world outlook can have on the rank-and-file federal investigators working day and night to prevent terrorist attacks. Agents with the best of intentions can be thwarted from advancing an investigation because of pressure to show that their motives are purely law-enforcement related and no judgment has been based on the subject's religion or appearance. This is specific to investigations into terror cases with a connection to radical Islam and creates an unnecessary layer of scrutiny based on the assumption that the good men and women investigating these types of cases would initiate a case based on a personal prejudice. It is this unnecessary, top-down politicization of an already heavily scrutinized federal investigative process that has real-world consequences. Often, those staffers who work in the insulated, crystal kingdom of Washington, DC, consistently fail to recognize the challenges of the agents doing the day-to-day work. This is one more instance of the dangerous effects that proliferating bureaucracy has on individuals within the government who are simply trying to do their jobs.

The Boston Marathon bombing was unprecedented in a number of unfortunate ways that I believe will permanently alter the domestic security landscape and hopefully change the dangerous path we are currently walking.

Terror attacks initiated by individuals of Chechen origin are an anomaly in the West. The Chechen separatist movement, seeking autonomy for Chechnya from the Russian federation, has avoided targeting the West, and specifically the United States, for strategic reasons. The Chechens have historically viewed us as geopolitical foes of the Russians and have not conducted attacks against us to avoid drawing us into their regional fight on the side of the Russians. Giving the US a reason to align with the Russians and rally behind a shared cause would be a tactical disaster for the separatist movement. The old saying "the enemy of my enemy is my friend" applies to the Chechen view of the United States.

However, this terrorist attack was not carried out by Chechen separatists, known for their ferocity in their attacks against the Russians. It was planned and executed by two brothers of Chechen descent who fled their homeland and integrated into the community in Boston, attending local schools, participating in social and athletic events, and, in the case of the older brother, even marrying an American woman.

The Tsarnaev brothers used the compassionate clause in American immigration law for political refugees seeking asylum and the generosity of the American social safety net to finance an attack against the country that gave them a chance at a better life. Photos of older brother Tamerlan in his flashy clothes and stories of him driving around his neighborhood in expensive cars are striking in their ideological hypocrisy. This ideological disconnect has real consequences for intelligence gathering as well because, in a prosperous country such as ours, young adults with flashy clothes and expensive cars are the exception and not the rule. These two brothers were living a middle-class existence in an average middle-class American neighborhood. Had they suddenly abandoned all of their material luxuries to pursue a perverse ideological war against our political and economic freedoms, then they would have likely elicited a greater degree of public suspicion. But the Tsarnaev brothers maintained a "normal" appearance to their neighbors and friends. They are not what we consider the traditional face of terror, and this made the case even more shocking.

Although major sporting events within the United States have long been coveted targets for international terrorist groups, no international group or individual has been successful at executing a terrorist plot at one. The 1996 Olympic Park bombing in Atlanta that killed one and injured over a hundred was actually carried out by a United States citizen,

Eric Rudolph. And, most damaging, with nothing more than small arms, smokeless powder, homemade shrapnel, and two pressure cookers, a teen and a twentysomething managed to effectively shut down a major United States city for nearly an entire business week and terrorize its entire population.

The Boston Marathon bombing was the first successful attack on American soil where surveillance camera technology and the controversial growth in its deployment directly contributed to the apprehension of the attackers before they were able to engage in additional destruction. This will inevitably advance the continuing national debate about the trade-offs between liberty and security as a growing number of Americans become uncomfortable with the new "surveillance society."

If there was a "new normal" in the aftermath of the terrorist attacks of September 11, 2001, then I believe we are in a "*new* new normal" after the April 15, 2013, Boston attack. It is clear now that, despite political statements to the contrary, global terrorist organizations are not "on the run" and are simply developing new operational models to deliver their product: terror.

Although the casualties and property damage resulting from the Boston attack were far less than those of 9/11, the long-term consequences are potentially more severe. The September 11 attacks utilized a "franchise" model of terrorism where cells of individuals, similar to franchisees in the business world, received training and guidance from an umbrella organization but implemented the destructive plan themselves. This contrasts with the Boston attack, in which the Tsarnaev brothers seemed to have been untrained and without support after the bombing. It is clear that someone taught them how to make the bombs, but the fact that they did not try to escape after the attack and carried it out without trying to disguise themselves shows a lack of sponsorship from a larger terrorist organization.

The tragic tactical success of the Boston attack has demonstrated to the world the potential for a new, more dangerous model of terrorism. I call it "sole proprietorship" terrorism.

Leveraging the explosive growth in online video sharing and social media, terrorist umbrella organizations can initiate the "self-radicalization" process through online jihadist propaganda and provide guidance and training through instructional content without ever having to get their hands dirty. Then, after a successful attack, the umbrella organization can use the event as marketing for new recruits.

This model is a greater danger because the self-radicalized members (or small groups in the case of the Tsarnaevs) have limited incriminating links and will leave fewer investigative and intelligence clues about the planning and operational stages of their attacks, making them harder to detect and prevent. Adding to the difficulty is the trend toward the expansion of the already segmented federal law-enforcement bureaucracy. Sole-proprietorship terrorism by nature does not involve the networks of individuals the franchise model relies on, and it will reduce the potential that these terrorists will somehow be flagged.

One example of the fragmentation among federal agencies comes from my experience in the Melville field office in conjunction with a bank fraud investigation. Although the investigation was initially referred to the Secret Service as a bank fraud case, as it unfolded and my target's network of contacts materialized, it became clear that members of his network were targets of other agencies' investigative antiterrorism efforts. This connection was uncovered by coincidence and not due to interagency operability.

The situation demanded that I contact the respective agencies and we work together to advance the investigation and apprehend the individuals. The cooperation was unnecessarily difficult at times because of the clashing of the bureaucracies involved, but eventually we accomplished our mission. When there is no network or cell, or the group is small and localized and its connection to the larger network is through cyberspace, the trail of investigative warning signs dries up. As leads become harder to follow and the interagency communication and information trading becomes more challenging and stressful, the fragmented nature of the investigative bodies can result in a sole-proprietor terrorist never being detected at all, as we saw in Boston.

A sole proprietor may make only a limited number of contacts that would be of investigative interest compared to the larger franchise cells that generate much more chatter. If any of these limited opportunities are missed, the chances of stopping an attack may be lost. Of course, information trading among agencies would be unnecessary if there were not so many different federal law-enforcement agencies acting as their own independent enterprises and contributing to the growing bureaucratic fog. The explosive growth of interagency segmentation and bureaucratic layering within agencies, in conjunction with the growing potential for sole-proprietor terrorism and limited investigative bread crumbs left on the trail, are significant factors working against government initiatives to combat terrorism.

We witnessed this exact phenomenon play out in the aftermath of the Boston attack, as details emerged about investigative clues about the attackers that were missed. Again, these missed clues were not due to any lack of dedication and mission focus by the individual federal agents who were involved, but by a broken and overly bureaucratic, multilayered federal law-enforcement structure.

The way the system works now, each agency exists primarily to protect its own turf, and the many layers within the agencies exist to protect the layer above, diffusing responsibility so no one is really responsible for the outcome of the game. The Boston Marathon case reminds me of the fraud investigation I conducted during my short tenure in the Baltimore field office. We found a number of co-conspirators in the target's network that I would uncover as the investigation progressed. Each time I entered a subject into the Secret Service's antiquated database and another Secret Service agent was interested in that subject, a message would appear with the agent's phone number and his case number. As a matter of standard investigative practice, I looked into the investigating agent's case for background information using the same system and would follow up with a detailed phone call to make the connections and put together the pieces of the investigative puzzle.

If this data-sharing process I described sounds simple, that's because it was. Even with an antiquated system like the one the Secret Service had at the time, agents were still able to find the information they needed and the contacts necessary to move the investigation forward. Compare this old, poorly funded system to the multibillion-dollar investigation into the radicalization of Tamerlan Tsarnaev by current federal law enforcement. His name was entered into numerous databases, including the FBI's Guardian Database, the Terrorist Identities Datamart Environment (TIDES), the Terrorist Screening Database (TSDB), and the Treasury Enforcement Communication System (TECS), which is managed by US Customs and Border Protection. Even with a search through all these sophisticated data platforms, federal law enforcement failed to produce any interagency investigative communication of value, and innocent American lives were lost as a result.

After the Boston Marathon attack, we learned that the Russian FSB (the former KGB) had already notified the FBI of Tamerlan's suspected radicalization in March of 2011. The FBI conducted a preliminary investigation that didn't produce anything of significance and concluded in June of 2011. The Russian FSB then notified the CIA of Tamerlan's suspected radical ties in September of 2011. Tamerlan traveled to Russia in January of 2012, causing an alert to initiate within the TECS database, and he returned to Boston from Russia in July 2012, initiating another TECS alert.

Why were the alerts not followed up on? The answer to this question is simple: too many agencies, too many databases, and too many competing agendas. The expansion in bureaucracy at the expense of agents in the field who are laser-focused on counterterrorism only serves to diffuse responsibility among the bureaucratic layers, none of which are incentivized to actually produce an answer and be accountable for the American lives lost and traumatized by a terror attack.

The American public must demand a real set of solutions to this problem. Having worked inside this bureaucratic fog, I am consistently confused as to why no one is seriously proposing an obvious solution that would fix these issues: a streamlined, decompartmentalized federal law-enforcement organization, under one umbrella, with one person at the top responsible for its mission.

This umbrella organization could be organized by the various law-enforcement specialties (financial crimes, drug enforcement, counterterrorism, diplomatic protection, etc.), and the problems of communication and information sharing between agencies would be replaced by far less serious intra-agency squabbles, which are more easily fixed. Under one agency, databases could be merged and access to them refined and expanded. The elimination of redundant missions would open up personnel for reassignment based on national priorities. The suffocating layers of management would be eliminated and strict accountability chains created. Office space could be downsized, and equipment and sophisticated law-enforcement laboratories could be combined for "one-stop shopping." The thousands of duplicative federal administrative forms that accomplish the same goal through redundant agency administrative paths would be eliminated and, most importantly, a new era of accountability would begin.

In addition to needing a complete reorganization of our federal law-enforcement bureaucracy, I believe new models of security need to evolve. The threat of terrorism is not going to disappear anytime soon, despite the current administration's belief that evil is purely a product of societal failings. I would strenuously argue that the long history of humankind refutes that premise. Violence has always been about a raw display of power, and the reasons humans can find for engaging in violence are too numerous to count. There is a disturbing but very real power in violence for someone who feels disenfranchised or to whom society has not provided economic power or the power of prestige and societal acceptance that accompany success. When society has left you behind, for whatever reason, either due to your own failings or circumstances beyond your control, you will seek some meaning for what has become a meaningless existence. That meaning may come from the group acceptance of a gang, the personal empowerment of violence at the expense of others, or a perverse ideological platform that provides an explanation for your own failings. Jihadist propaganda, readily available in a world made small by the growth in Internet communication, will become that platform for increasing numbers of the world's Tsarnaev brothers, in search of a cause and a way to make their statement to the world.

It is not surprising to the intelligence or law-enforcement communities that jihadist propaganda would appeal to a segment of our society, and that self-radicalization is not only possible but very likely for some of our own citizens. The rigors of daily American life, as well as our responsibilities to our families and our jobs, lend order and structure to our lives and eliminate the need to pursue violent propaganda. We tend to view the world as a series of actions and consequences, and the idea of engaging in deadly violence to further a cause is repulsive to most of us. But violence to achieve an ideological goal, however repulsive to civilized men and women, has been the norm for most of human existence. The ability to use force to subjugate people you perceive as your enemies or to take what you desire, whether earned or not, is quite natural, and the power achieved can reinforce that kind of behavior. It is our unprecedented level of prosperity, and the corresponding fulfillment of most of our fundamental needs as humans, that make this idea of "violence as natural" so foreign to us.

This presents an obvious danger for a society looking to prevent terrorists from causing the mass chaos they caused in Boston. Once again, the franchise model of terrorism requires interaction, and each interaction leaves a ripple that if detected could be used to investigate and thwart an attack. One person acting alone will not leave as many of these ripples and has a substantially greater chance of avoiding detection. Sadly, this is likely to result in a new series of security measures and encroachments on individual liberties that we are not accustomed to in the United States. These encroachments will not be voluntary and will inevitably change the way we view public events in the future. Subjecting yourself to a frisk at a public event may become standard operating procedure, and security cameras will proliferate to the point where any public area of a major city will likely be monitored.

The New Year's Eve celebration in Times Square and the presidential inauguration are examples of high-profile outdoor events with large crowds that have successfully implemented security plans that have kept all participants safe to date. The security models used by the New York City Police Department and Secret Service for these events will most likely be the standard going forward. These events attract millions of revelers and despite some setbacks they have never had a major security breach. Security officials accomplish this by creating "access zones" where the public can view the event. Similar to the "box within a box" approach I described earlier in the book, these models do not attempt to do the impossible.

During a number of interviews I conducted prior to the 2012 presidential inauguration, I was asked, "How does the Secret Service secure the entire city for the inauguration?" The answer is: they don't. The same approach is applied to the city of Washington that I used at the Caterpillar factory visit that I coordinated for President Obama. The factory was full of dangerous equipment and chemicals, so we built a "box" within the factory and focused our limited assets on securing that limited area. The DC Metro police and other law-enforcement agencies can secure the streets of Washington, DC, but the Secret Service PPD has to secure the president's location only. During the inauguration we accomplished this by utilizing strategically placed barriers to ensure that people who entered locations where they would be close to the president did so only through specific "people-funnel" checkpoints.

For a presidential inauguration we insist that everyone pass through a metal detector, but this is not necessary to substantially reduce the risk of another Boston-type attack. The Boston bombers were carrying anti-personnel improvised explosives devices (IEDs) designed to kill or maim large numbers of people and inspire fear. In order to carry out that type of attack, you need a dense crowd in which to detonate the device. If the Boston Police Department had a plan in place for the marathon similar to the NYPD's Times Square plan, where anyone accessing such areas as the starting line, the halfway point, and the finish line, where people tend to congregate, was subject to a bag check and quick pat-down in lieu of metal detectors, the attackers would have been forced to rethink their plans.

It troubles me to have to suggest a "new normal" way of life in our country because of the evaporation of individual liberty that will result as a consequence of increased security. So far lawmakers have not made any progress in revising laws that protect individual freedoms and the right to privacy. Provisions within poorly written sections of the PATRIOT Act, for example, have been misused and will continue to be until the law is refined. In addition, the billions of dollars spent on federalizing airport security have consistently failed to produce the desired results, while subjecting the public to frustrating, often embarrassing security screenings.

A lesson to take from this move toward a surveillance state is that no security measure comes without a trade-off. As Israeli major general and terror expert Amos Yadlin has stated, "it's not the tools but the rules of engagement." The PATRIOT Act was a tool with poorly defined rules of engagement that were left open to law enforcement's interpretation. When the rules are open to interpretation, law enforcement will always seek the broadest interpretation to make their case. It is not personal; the men and women of the federal law-enforcement community whom I have worked with are members of our wider communities—fathers, mothers, neighbors, soccer coaches—and have no personal interest in violating your liberty. They are simply working with a set of imperfect tools.

The same can be said for expanding the use of surveillance cameras. There is nothing inherently evil about surveillance cameras, but when government officials are unclear about the rules of engagement as to where these cameras will be placed, why they will be placed there, and what will be done with the footage, Americans grow understandably concerned. From my experience, surveillance is nonthreatening only to those doing the watching, not those being watched.

23

OUR GOVERNMENT HAS FAILED US

DURING MY RUN for the United States Senate I learned that in the business of politics, themes are important. Themes are helpful because they assist your audience in both understanding and categorizing the information you are trying to get across to them. A theme should speak to a larger idea but be compact enough to remember.

If I had to sum up the theme of this book, it would be "beware of the soft tyranny of bureaucracies."

When *everyone* has responsibility for something as critical as security and emergency response, then *no one* has ultimate responsibility. Having lived inside the bubble, I have seen for myself how our government has grown to such a point where decision makers can take credit for politically beneficial outcomes and hide behind the false facade of "the bureaucracy" when scandal and tragedy strike. There is no moral difference between the hard tyranny of acting against the citizens you swore to serve and the soft tyranny of hiding like a coward and allowing someone under your chain of command to take the fall.

The events and experiences I described in these final few chapters were specifically chosen to show the contrast between individual sacrifice and dedication, and the systematic failures of our current government. I was constantly awed by the many men and women I worked with during my time as a Secret Service agent and their dedication to their mission. It is challenging to reconcile how some federal employees can be so selfless when others are completely out of touch with the country they are supposed to serve.

The problem with our government is not the people but the system that fosters a "just following orders" approach and marginalizes good people attempting to do the right thing. A perfect example is the recent Benghazi hearings, where whistle-blowers finally were allowed to testify after enduring months of intimidation and threats by those in the administration who did not want the truth to be told. We are rapidly approaching the point where we must ask ourselves if we want a limited, smaller government that performs a small number of tasks well, or an expansive government that performs a large portfolio of tasks poorly. The consequences of the wrong choice are very real, as I have documented in the recent tragedies in Arizona, Benghazi, and Boston.

I was privileged during my twelve years with the United States Secret Service and my four years with the New York City Police Department to work with local, state, and federal officials from the law enforcement, legislative, judicial, prosecutorial, diplomatic, and military divisions within our system of government. I found bravery, honor, and sense of duty to be the rule, not the exception. Although government employment can provide for a solid middle-class existence, no one is going to become wealthy as a government employee. Despite this unavoidable economic fact, some of the brightest, hardest-working people I have ever encountered have decided that service to the government and the American people was their proper path.

This begs the important question: how is it that a government populated with hard-working, dedicated men and women applying their intellectual and physical gifts to public service could produce law enforcement, security, and counterterrorism failures such as Fast and Furious, Benghazi, and the Boston bombings?

The answer lies in bureaucratic failure. In the example of Fast and Furious, the government's failure to slow the proliferation of illegal firearm sales by prosecuting the case in a timely manner appears nearly criminal. As I describe in my analysis, I place the blame squarely on the Department of Justice. It is not the people within the department who have failed, but the system they work within that is broken. The incentives within the system have been perverted as a result of the growth in the levels of bureaucracy within the DOJ and the politicization of its agenda. Rather than being incentivized to prioritize and fight criminality with the greatest negative impact on American citizens, the incentives are set up to prosecute cases that are neatly packaged by investigators in order to give federal prosecutors easy guilty verdicts. This is done to avoid lengthy trials and potentially losing the case, which would negatively affect both the DOJ's budget and prosecutorial success rate. Do not underestimate the impact of these factors—many cases with merit whose investigation and prosecution would make our country substantially safer are bypassed or delayed due to bureaucratic ineptitude and crass political considerations, not personal failures. Forcing a system of unethical incentives on individuals, regardless of the content of their character, is inevitably corrupting.

This broken system being forced upon the federal agents and employees working within it undoubtedly played a role in the numerous failures leading to the Benghazi attacks. It is assumed that our government has a moral requirement to do everything in its power to defend those serving the country overseas. So how do we explain the lack of assistance to those who came under assault with the imminent threat of serious personal injury or death? How do we excuse it when someone in government ignores desperate pleas for help just to save a political career?

Based on my experience within the walls of the White House, I am confident that a number of military, diplomatic, law-enforcement, and

Obama administration officials were well aware of the SOS signal from the heroes in Benghazi and the danger of their situation. Yet they were left to die.

Not only were their pleas ignored but, based on the accounts of a number of contacts I have spoken to, the military unit that was initially activated to rescue the Benghazi victims was instructed to stand down. It is simply not possible that all the eyes and ears that saw and heard the pleas of Ambassador Stevens and his team all belonged to people lacking a moral compass who did not care about the victims. These people were likely forced into compliance by a top-down decision-making process that was driven by politics first and the safety of the personnel in Benghazi a distant second. The penalty for failing to "go along" was and is severe. Jobs may have been threatened, and this is a sad testament to where we have come as a government.

Growing levels of bureaucracy in all areas of our government have made it possible to deflect the deadly consequences of decisions. The blame can be spread thin as a result of the diffusion of responsibility that comes with the explosive expansion of the bureaucratic class. The "I was just following orders" phenomenon is facilitated by a bureaucracy so large that even senior-level diplomatic officials comprised only a small part of the decision-making pie. It allows these officials to tell themselves that although the decision to abandon those men and let them die in Benghazi was both morally and legally bankrupt and a violation of their oath to support and defend the Constitution, it was not theirs alone and they were "just following orders." This was even stated by the State Department's own politically driven Accountability Review Board, assigned to investigate the Benghazi terror attacks, when it concluded that "systemic failures and leadership and management deficiencies at senior levels within two bureaus of the State Department . . . resulted in a Special Mission security posture that was inadequate for Benghazi and grossly inadequate to deal with the attack that took place. Security in Benghazi was not recognized and implemented as a shared responsibility by the bureaus in Washington charged with supporting the post, resulting in fragmented discussions and decisions on policy and security." It is also noted in the report that "certain senior State Department officials within two bureaus in critical positions of authority and responsibility in Washington demonstrated a lack of proactive leadership and management ability."

The broken system unfortunately surfaces again in the missed opportunities to disrupt the Boston terror attacks. Despite an analysis done after the 9/11 attacks that conclusively stated that interagency government communications were severely lacking and contributed greatly to a number of missed opportunities to break up the 9/11 terrorists' operation while in the planning stages, we still suffer from the same problem and failed again with the Boston terror suspects.

Again, this is not a function of an army of federal law-enforcement officials who do not take seriously their solemn responsibilities to the American people; it is a function of a system set up to fail and minimize the effects of anyone looking to change it. No organization can overcome the effects of having over a hundred thousand federal law-enforcement officials isolated within different fiefdoms of government. All of these government agencies have different communications networks, investigative priorities, budget priorities, and cultures that, at times, run directly counter to the missions of their brother agencies. We saw in the Fast and Furious investigation that we had ATF agents investigating suspected gunrunners who were, unbeknownst to the ATF, working as informants for the FBI. In the Benghazi attacks, we had a politically driven Accountability Review Board conclude—seemingly blind to the fact that we have tens of thousands of federal agents currently investigating low-priority crimes—that resource constraints "had the effect of conditioning a few State Department managers to favor restricting the use of resources as a general orientation." And finally, we had a terror suspect, Tamerlan Tsarnaev, exit the country, setting off what Department of Homeland Security secretary Janet Napolitano called a "ping" in the DHS computer system, which the FBI was unaware of and led to no investigative follow-up. Secretary Napolitano never describes the "ping" because she likely does not understand what the "ping" means either.

Any private citizen can set up a Google Alert and receive an e-mail the instant his name appears on the Internet, but incredibly, our behemoth federal government has yet to figure out how to keep track of terrorists who freely come in and out of our country. If this sounds like an oversimplification, I assure you it is not. The dense fog of bureaucracy has descended on our government, and wading through it to find your path

is more and more difficult. I remember my early days with the Secret
Service working in the Melville field office when I was actively engaged
in the investigation of a fraud ring with a distinct connection to terrorism.
I involved the FBI's local office because of the terrorism angle and was
taken aback at having to make an appointment to drive over to their office
and take physical custody of a document on one of the suspects that was
redacted (blacked out) to the point where it was almost unreadable. I had
a top-secret clearance and was authorized to carry a firearm next to the
president of the United States in order to protect him and his family, but
apparently I was not trusted to read another agency's document regarding
a suspect I was investigating. The delays in the investigation due to this
web of obstacles were substantial and serve as a small example of the large
problem we face in an ever-expanding government.

I was honored to serve my country as a special agent with the Secret
Service, but living within the bubble of Washington, DC, leaves scars that
are a permanent reminder of a broken system—a system that incentivizes
acquiescence at the expense of both the American public and the dedicated
cadre of federal employees who largely sought out public service as a means
to serve, not harm, their fellow Americans.

I saw this numerous times in my career and distinctly recall asking
why we transferred agents around the country to different field offices at
great financial cost despite any obvious need for it. I was told, "That's the
way we have always done it."

As the late economist Milton Friedman once stated, "When everybody
owns something, nobody owns it, and nobody has a direct interest in
maintaining or improving its condition."

Although Friedman was referring to property, the principle of which
he speaks is perfectly applicable to the fact that our ever-expanding
government has created a system where very few people have any direct
personal interest in improving its functioning. It is ironic that some
political opportunists have sold the American public on the idea that a
growing government means a more caring, benevolent government and
a more prosperous society. The sad reality is that a growing government
has led to a more callous, detached government, where the diffusion of
responsibility throughout the exploding legions of new bureaucrats has
led to bad decision making.

We can fix this, but it is going to require a new era of citizen activism, an activism where we take responsibility for a better government and we stop relying on those inside the bubble to fix the mess they have created. Call the offices of your elected officials until you receive the answers you are looking for. Show up at town hall meetings and refuse to be silenced until your questions are answered. Write letters to your local newspapers challenging the status quo. Use the power of social media to spread your message. Do not remain silent, because silence is complicity.

But most important of all, do not lose hope. This country is exceptional because it is not simply a group of people or a piece of land—it is the embodiment of an idea. It is an idea that heroic men and women for generations have fought and died for, sacrificing their lives knowing that our incomparable American freedom and our exceptional degree of individual liberty were unique to this place. We can fix this; we can turn this ship around. But it all begins with you.

AFTERWORD

THE IDEA FOR THIS BOOK came about because of a paradox I encountered during my time with the Secret Service. Having worked with legions of dedicated and patriotic military personnel, federal law-enforcement agents, and political staffers who genuinely cared about their country and its citizens, I wondered why a government composed of genuinely good people continues to get it wrong. In light of the bevy of scandals that broke subsequent to the completion of this book, the question has become even more pressing.

My answer to this question is made clear in the final chapters, where I state that the growing government bureaucracy has diffused responsibility both vertically and horizontally so that the idea of responsibility has lost all of its meaning. When everyone takes a small bite of the decision-making pie, no one is really responsible when the baker asks, "Who ate my pie?"

The recent scandal within the Internal Revenue Service, where ideologically conservative groups were targeted by the agency, is yet another troubling example of this phenomenon. I have no doubt that the employees who were instructed to target these groups felt that by the time the orders to do so reached their desks, it must have been legal and in compliance with agency regulations given the many layers of bureaucratic management that they perceived as vetting the decision. This troubling development should serve as a wake-up call to every American to demand change from a government they finance through tax dollars earned through their hard work. Being targeted by a government you have paid for is a moral travesty, and unfortunately the trend line, under the current conditions of seemingly endless bureaucratic growth, is moving in the wrong direction.

The IRS is not the only government agency that has landed on the front pages due to scandal. The leaks about the monitoring of Americans by our National Security Agency is another example of this paradox. Living in Maryland, I have been surrounded by employees of the NSA for many years, and I can personally attest to their individual commitment to the United States of America and the principles of freedom. Yet they have been instructed by their management to comply with a program that breaks down the essential contract between US citizens and their government that has made the United States the greatest country in the long history of civilized man. The central tenet of that contract is a liberty based on the principle that the line between the private and the public self is drawn by the citizen, not the government. In totalitarian regimes, there is no private self. Everyone is a potential agent of the government, and informing on your neighbor is encouraged to ensure that every citizen understands that he is part of a "collective." Such an environment can be enforced only when there is no wall between the individual and the government. In our unique, liberty-loving society, that essential contract—that the freedom of the individual has primacy over the authority of the state—has led us to the greatest standard of living and the most prosperous conditions in human history.

When we leave the house each morning and open our front doors, we have made a conscious decision to leave the private self behind and allow the world to see the public self again, a line drawn by us. These are always going to be different masks that we all wear, the private and the public one. The common retort I hear from defenders of government monitoring is, "If you are doing nothing wrong, you have nothing to be concerned about." My experience inside the bubble has conclusively led me to believe that this is a nonsensical argument. We all do something wrong sometimes, since we are all fallible human beings. As long as our private "wrongs" do not impact on the civil liberties of others and do not violate any laws, control of when and if they are made public should be the exclusive domain of the individual, not the government.

To accentuate this point, I want to share a hypothetical example that sounds unlikely only to those who place a blind trust in their government. It is only a matter of time before an innocent American who may have information of value to the government—information he thought was private—sees it used against him as leverage to get him to cooperate. The point is not whether he should or should not cooperate but that information he thought was the exclusive purview of the private self in a free society was not private at all, and it was the government that made that determination. This will fracture the fabric of our free society and make us all unwilling accomplices to an ongoing federal investigation that could have been solved using the methods I describe in this book's final chapters rather than collecting the private communications of millions of individuals.

My years of experience with information and the government lead me to believe that when you forfeit your personal information without a fight, it will be abused. It is only a matter of when, not if.

Turning the trend line back toward liberty is going to require a new degree of citizen activism. Apathy is the weapon of choice for the supporters of these government intrusions into your private life. In my experience, there is nothing that disturbs the White House or Congress more than a flood of calls to the switchboard on a particular issue. This requires a commitment from the electorate to take the time to make these calls to their elected representatives and to demand a change in direction.

Please do not fall victim to the "one person cannot make a difference" meme. Rosa Parks, Martin Luther King, Jr., and the army of American citizens who took to the streets during the struggle for civil rights refused to accept the status quo and changed the course of American history for the better. You can make a difference if you commit yourself to action. The only power in words is to motivate people to action. A better tomorrow awaits your response.

INDEX

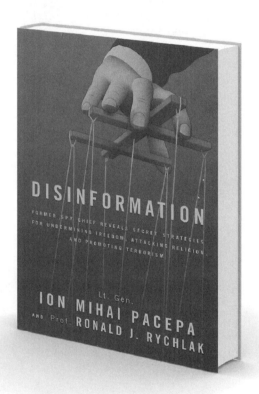
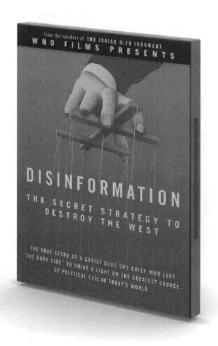

PRESENTS

THE BOOK THAT CAN CHANGE THE COURSE OF OUR NATION.

Far from a collection of generalized gripes concerning Barack Obama and his administration, *Impeachable Offenses* dispassionately rolls out the case for the indictment of a president based upon specific, major violations of law and the Constitution.

PRESENTS

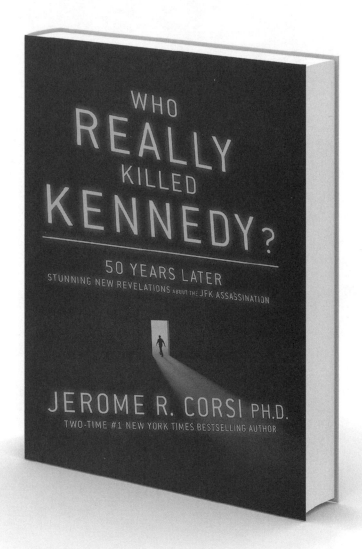

New York Times bestselling author Jerome R. Corsi, Ph.D., provides readers with the ultimate JFK assassination theory book. One-by-one, each chapter examines the strongest arguments regarding the killing of JFK, including theories surrounding the mob, the CIA, Cuban radicals, LBJ, right-wing extremists and more.

WND Books

P R E S E N T S

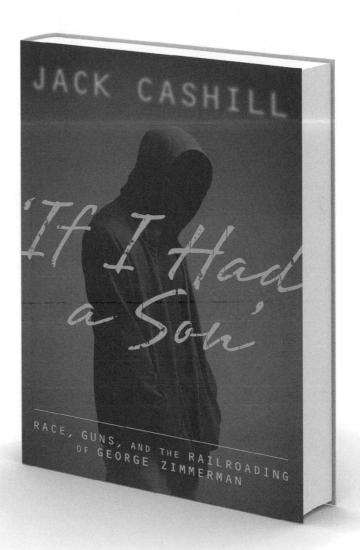

In *'If I Had A Son'*, Jack Cashill tells the inside story of how, as the result of a tragic encounter with troubled seventeen-year-old Trayvon Martin, the media turned Tugboat into a white racist vigilante, "the most hated man in America."